BUILDING CAREER EQUITY

How professionals and their firms achieve
mutual and meaningful growth

2nd
EDITION

JAN TORRISI-MOKWA

CONGRUENCE
PRESS

ISBN: 978-0-9831896-0-2

Book designed by Nehmen-Kodner: n-kcreative.com
Printed in the United States of America

Published by: Congruence Press
www.buildingcareerequity.com • email: jan@congruence-inc.com

To all those who make the choice, every day, to dream, learn, work, collaborate, give, and recognize others in pursuit of realizing their career aspirations.

Contents

Introduction

The concept of Career Equity developed when I was at Arthur Andersen. The firm, like all professional service firms, experienced a high rate of turnover (nearly 24 percent) of its best and brightest associates. A strategic managing partner understood the correlation between high levels of effective client service and retention of top talent. Over the next three years, we worked with the firm's partners to erase double-digit turnover and build a culture of growth that benefitted each professional and the firm's business results. The process is repeatable, timeless and it works.

Culture building began by interviewing professionals at every level of the firm — those new to the firm, equity partners, staff, and most importantly, those who left or were thinking of leaving. Each meeting helped me better understand what compelled professionals to stay or go. Concurrently, we analyzed every one of the firm's people processes (e.g., recruiting, on-boarding, training and development, and performance evaluation). We studied what professionals' valued and which practices were unintentionally reinforcing an expectation of early career turnover. Three key issues emerged from the research.

First, fewer than 10 percent of professionals had a career vision. After completing the two-year experience requirement and achieving the credential of Certified Public Accountant (CPA), the majority of professionals had no clear long-term plan. We learned that when achievement-oriented professionals lack a career vision, it undermines their ability to make effective career choices in the present.

Second, we learned that when new career opportunities or dissatisfaction with a current experience emerged, professionals did not naturally seek the counsel of a partner or owner who could affect a change in their situation. Rather, they sought guidance from peers or significant others. While seeking feedback from friends and family may seem logical and helpful, it is not optimal for making strategic career decisions. Family and friends do not have the power, influence, or authority to change career conditions. In other words, unless you are in a family-owned business, peers and family do not control your pay, progression, or assignments. Thus, the people who needed most to talk with each other (professionals and partners) were not doing so.

Finally, we learned that the firm's people-related business processes were not strategically integrated to help professionals see the relationship between their initial career goals, mentoring programs, training investments, and performance feedback, or most importantly, the link to firm business results. In other words, how an individual's hard work contributed to firm success was vague. Significant time and resources were expended on these initiatives, however, prior to the Career Equity model they managed to achieve separate results. When a professional can't see the whole picture or how the firm seeks to help them advance, the firm's ability to leverage these investments diminishes. Over several years of defining and implementing the Building Career Equity model we achieved a triple win. First, professional turnover dropped from 24 percent to less than 14 percent. This result occurred at the peak of the dot.com "War for Talent," not during an economic recession. Second, professionals had higher levels of satisfaction and a strategy they could discuss with partners and career advisors. Last, the career-oriented integrated framework improved our ability to attract new talent and better serve clients. We stopped the "revolving door" and provided greater continuity on client engagements.

Professionals could see the value of their career experiences grow in tangible ways and clients did not have new people on their account every six months. Additionally, the firm's best people were watching. When they saw partners taking a sincere interest in the career growth of others, they were more proactive about sharing their career aspirations. Career decisions that were once isolated became more collaborative. A virtuous cycle of growth was created and sustained.

Today, the issues professionals face in defining and achieving their long-term career goals remain the same, and caring firm leaders are still in pursuit of win-win solutions. The firms that are named as applying "best practices" in Chapter 8 utilized the lessons learned at Andersen and successfully applied them to their own culture. Their results have been equally significant.

If you are a professional seeking greater career growth, I hope this book serves as a catalyst for you to think, discern, and most importantly, take action on proven strategies that have helped other professionals achieve more of their career goals. If you are a firm leader, harness the lessons learned and make professional career growth part of your firm's business strategy. Either way, enjoy. If you find value, commit to teaching these practices to others. As Stephen R. Covey helped me realize, teaching others leads to the highest level of self-awareness and effectiveness.

1: What Is Your Career Equity?

"If one advances confidently in the direction of his dreams, and endeavors to live the life which he has imagined, he will meet with a success unexpected in common hours."

—Henry David Thoreau

f you are reading this book, it is likely that someone who cares about you recommended it, or you found it researching strategies to enhance career growth. In either case, you are a Career Equity builder.

What Is Your Career Equity?

Career Equity is a way of thinking, a framework, or paradigm about your career. It resonates most with those who possess or aspire to a calling requiring special knowledge and intense academic preparation. In short, anyone who considers him or herself a professional and is deliberate about building a meaningful career is accumulating Career Equity.

Building Career Equity offers a set of proven steps to increase clarity, career satisfaction and provides tools that when implemented consistently accelerate the value of your career. It inspires professionals to evaluate how career investments are adding up and where opportunities exist to increase career effectiveness. We know professionals spend as much as 60 percent of their waking life at work, yet fewer than 20 percent use systematic and strategic tools to manage their careers. When was the last time you sat down and reviewed all of your accomplishments and career aspirations with a career advisor? In financial matters, a disciplined process of planning, researching, working with a trusted advisor, and plan implementation leads to greater results. Those who implement Career Equity discover the same rewards in their careers. Why is it that more than 80 percent of professionals do not have long-term written career plans or regularly review them with an advisor? I believe most professionals lack a holistic and systematic way of thinking about their career as do their career advisors.

Most of us manage our careers incrementally. We evaluate career choices based on the opportunity in front of us. Shall I leave this firm? Do I like or dislike working with the leader in this practice? Career Equity helps us take a longer view. Career Equity builders envision their future careers and then design, document, and implement a comprehensive plan to achieve their desired results. They know that absent a framework for guiding career decisions, short-term external factors such as discontentment with a project, conflict with a manager or peers, or a competing salary offer can derail their long-term aspirations. While no plan is perfect and unplanned external factors (e.g., job loss due to economic downturns) do happen, Career

Equity builders take initiative and responsibility for career choices and avoid impulsive career changes and the regret of erratic career growth.

This book offers strategies to achieve more of the career growth and satisfaction you desire. When defined, reviewed, and implemented consistently, these lead to exceptional results. Your Career Equity is comprised of five assets: 1) Doing Engaging Work, 2) Cultivating Meaningful Relationships, 3) Relentlessly Pursuing Learning and Growth, 4) Contributing to Community, and 5) Reaping the Right Recognition and Rewards.

What follows are real-life stories, tools, strategies, and action plans for building Career Equity. Part of being an effective Career Equity builder begins with awareness of the daily choices you make to build and replenish one of the most important assets in your life. To get your career growth underway, let us begin with a few questions:

1) **Who do you know who does a great job of managing their career?** In other words, they are clear about where they want to go and work strategically to get there. Write down the top two or three people who embody these traits.

1. _____

2. _____

3. _____

2) What characteristics do these professionals demonstrate that you admire? What do they do that makes them come to mind and why are they so effective? Were any of the following on your list?

- Invest time on their career goals and plans.
- Define a compelling vision about where they want to be in the future.
- Seek out mentoring and feedback to learn and grow.
- Invest relentlessly in learning and developing new skills or knowledge.
- Give generously of their time and talent to build a better community or help others succeed.

Career Equity builders are strategic, thoughtful, engaged, and purposeful in managing most things in their life, especially their career. If you choose to fully implement the ideas and recommendations that follow, you will develop these characteristics and more. Reading and investing the time to think and act on your career aspirations in a new way means you are well on your way.

A Career Equity Builder Example

At 7:30 a.m. on a Saturday, I met with Tasha to discuss her next career opportunity. The meeting happened because Tasha took the initiative to arrange it. Tasha and I met initially when she was pursuing her undergraduate degree in human resources (HR) and I was the director of Human Resources at Arthur Andersen. She wanted to gain practical experience in HR through an internship and had come to me through a referral from a member of the local chapter of the Society of Human Resource Management (SHRM). I share these details because they are evidence of behaviors that determine those who achieve their career goals and those who do not. Thinking about future career goals, taking initiative to meet with a "trusted advisor," involvement in a professional organization, and pursuing skill development through an internship are all evidence of Career Equity building skills.

This particular morning, more than seven years after our initial connection, Tasha wanted to discuss an offer she received to work at The Boeing Company. Tasha was utilizing me as one of her **Career Board of Directors** (discussed in Chapter 2) to help her assess how this opportunity aligned with her longer-term goals and the best strategy for negotiating a salary and benefits that would be a win-win for her and the company.

We discussed how a career at The Boeing Company would help Tasha accumulate more Career Equity. She decided that this opportunity would give her experience in one of the world's largest and most reputable companies, access to world class learning experiences, and the challenge of developing and implementing people solutions in a dynamic organization and industry. Tasha had specific questions about how the Boeing culture might differ from her prior career experiences in smaller organizations and what she could do to effectively manage the transition to such a large company. A few days after our meeting, I received a heartfelt handwritten note from Tasha which expressed her gratitude for my time: another attribute of Career Equity builders. I also received a follow-up email from Tasha, outlining the key points she took away from our meeting and a plan for acting on the things we discussed. Kudos to Tasha for her excellent Career Equity building behavior. Without prompting or management from me, Tasha was in charge of her career. A few weeks later, I received another update from Tasha letting me know that she had accepted the position and was excited to begin this new dimension of her career. Whether you are looking for a new career opportunity or interested in expanding Career Equity in your current role and organization, Tasha's story is a great road map. Like Tasha, a good place to begin is to take stock of the equity you have already acquired and where you have the opportunity to increase your career growth. To gain a better understanding of your Career Equity, take a few moments and answer the following questions about your current career situation. The assessment results can also point to the chapters in the book most relevant to you now.

The Building Career Equity Assessment

The Building Career Equity Assessment (see pages 13-17) will help you identify where important career assets are accumulating and where opportunities exist to achieve a higher return. Since effective career growth never occurs in a vacuum, the completed assessment provides a practical tool for discussing career growth with interested managers, mentors, and advisors. Using a scale from 1 to 5; where 5 = very true for my career today, 3 = somewhat true for my career today, and 1 = not at all true for my career today, read each of the statements and place the appropriate rating in the box to the right of the statement. Then total the number of points at the end of each asset category. Follow the directions below to see what your Career Equity Assessment is telling you.

Career Equity Assessment In Action

Career Equity is achieved by purposeful action, persistence, and patience. The following is a guideline for evaluating your Career Equity and asset accumulation in each category.

What Your Scores Mean

- Scores between 45 and 50 in a category indicate an exceptional level of career investment and development.
- Scores that fall between 35 and 44 in a category indicate progressive career growth. You are advancing and building assets, but a little extra intention would take your investments to the next level.
- Scores that fall between 25 and 34 in a category indicate moderate Career Equity building. You would benefit from a higher level of focus and attention. Take the initiative to review your assessment with a career mentor or advisor in the next 30 days and formulate an action plan to work in one area immediately.

- Scores that fall between 25 and 34 in a category indicate moderate Career Equity building. You would benefit from a higher level of focus and attention. Take the initiative to review your assessment with a career mentor or advisor in the next 30 days and formulate an action plan to work in one area immediately.
- Any category total of 24 or less indicates low-asset return, a need for greater intention, planning, and accountability. Pick one asset area that demands attention and create a plan to increase the results in the next year. Review your plan monthly.

While exceptional scores in every area seem desirable, it is not typical. Those who are purposeful about building Career Equity over the long-term identify the vital few areas where they want to accumulate significant assets and work to do so! Consider the following questions:

- What stands out to you about the current state of your Career Equity?
- Which of the assets yielded the highest number of points?
- Which asset needs immediate attention?
- Which statement caught your attention?

Armed with greater awareness about where you are now, you can focus on where you want to be in the future and how to do more work that engages you.

The Building Career Equity Assessment	
Career Asset #1 **Doing Engaging Work**	**Scale of** **1–5**
1. My work challenges me intellectually, socially, and emotionally.	
2. I take initiative to seek out information about new projects and strategies my company or firm is pursuing.	
3. The work I do provides opportunities to gain new skills, knowledge, or experiences.	
4. I have a high level of variety in my work.	
5. I feel energized and enthusiastic about the work I do.	
6. I have a clear written vision for my career.	
7. I have a high degree of autonomy in my work.	
8. I have the right resources (materials, equipment, etc.).	
9. People I work with are concerned about the challenge my work offers.	
10. I know where my talents best fit the needs of the organization.	
Total Points for This Asset (50 possible)	

The Building Career Equity Assessment	
Career Asset #2 **Cultivating Meaningful Relationships**	**Scale of 1–5**
1. I care about the people with whom I work.	
2. I have a network of professionals who are willing to help me grow and learn.	
3. My opinion matters to others with whom I work.	
4. There is at least one person in my life who encourages my career growth.	
5. I have at least one best friend at work.	
6. In the past six months, I have taken the initiative to discuss my career goals with a leader in my company or firm.	
7. I have developed at least one mentor relationship where I work.	
8. I have developed at least one mentor outside my firm or company.	
9. I solicit open, honest feedback about my performance on a regular basis.	
10. I express gratitude in a tangible and meaningful way to those who invest in my growth.	
Total Points for This Asset (50 possible)	

The Building Career Equity Assessment	
Career Asset #3 **Relentlessly Pursuing Learning and Growth**	**Scale of** **1–5**
1. I read at least one book or magazine a month to advance my professional skills and knowledge.	
2. Each year, I create a professional growth and development plan with specific measurable goals for learning (e.g., 20 hours).	
3. I can articulate my strengths and the activities and projects that energize me at work.	
4. I know what differentiates me from other professionals in my area of expertise and am working to build this brand.	
5. In the past six months, I have taken the initiative to talk with someone about my professional development or learning goals.	
6. I serve as a teacher or facilitator by training others at least once a year.	
7. I complete a self-evaluation of my performance each year.	
8. I know my areas for development and have a written plan of action to develop them.	
9. My leaders help me identify work assignments or projects that address my areas for development.	
10. My training and development plan is linked to the strategic needs of the organization I work for or aspire to work for.	
Total Points for This Asset (50 possible)	

The Building Career Equity Assessment	
Career Asset #4 **Contributing to Community and Culture Scale**	**Scale of** **1–5**
1. The organization I work for is respected in the community.	
2. I can articulate the two or three ways I would like to make a difference in the world or my community.	
3. I have written goals for my community involvement this year.	
4. I am on the Board or committee of a non-profit organization.	
5. I invite others to participate in community activities or events.	
6. I have been recognized by a community organization for my efforts.	
7. I believe community involvement enhances career growth and progression.	
8. I solicit feedback from mentors/advisors on opportunities for community involvement.	
9. My employer has a clear Purpose/Mission and Values that align with my values.	
10. I attend an "off-hours" community event at least once a month.	
Total Points for This Asset (50 possible)	

The Building Career Equity Assessment	
Career Asset #5 **Reaping the Right Rewards and Recognition**	**Scale of** **1–5**
1. In the past month, I received recognition or praise for my work.	
2. I know the market value of pay and benefits for my position and experience.	
3. I use at least 70 percent or more of my annual vacation time each year.	
4. I participate in a 401K program or other retirement savings plan.	
5. I am fully informed about my health care benefits: medical, dental, life insurance, and long-term disability.	
6. I am satisfied with my level of base pay compensation.	
7. I have a high degree of flexibility in choosing when I take time off for vacation, etc.	
8. My organization makes contributions to charities or organizations I believe in.	
9. The people I work with want me to succeed and advance.	
10. In the past month, I have given recognition or praise to a co-worker.	
Total Points for This Asset (50 possible)	

Extra Credit

At the end of each chapter you will discover tools, ideas, and resources to accelerate the learning and application of the Career Equity building process. Here are a few to get you started:

1) Share the Career Equity assessment with a friend or colleague. Ask them to complete the assessment, and compare results.

2) Share your Career Equity assessment results and action plan with a coach or mentor. Get their feedback on next steps.

3) Read *How to Find the Work You Love,* Lawrence G. Boldt, (New York: Penguin Group, 1996) or *Discovering Your Career in Business,* Timothy Butler and James Waldroop, (New York: Perseus Books, 1996).

2: Doing Engaging Work

"Being busy does not mean real work. The object of all work is accomplishment and to this end there must be forethought, system, planning, intelligence, and honest purpose, as well as perspiration. Seeming to do is not doing."

—*Thomas A. Edison*

What Work Most Energizes And Engages You?

Mihály Csíkszentmihályi, in his seminal work, *Flow: The Psychology of Optimal Experience*, reveals that people experience superb satisfaction when they are in a state of *flow*. Flow is a state of concentration or complete absorption with an activity in which the person is fully immersed and has a feeling of energized focus and full engagement. Time flies. Every action, movement, and thought follows inevitably from the previous one. In flow, the emotions are not just channeled, but positive, energized, and aligned with the task at hand. Does the work that you do produce flow? What percent of the time do your professional experiences bring satisfaction, energy, and enthusiasm? Building Career Equity is about increasing the percentage of time you realize career engagement or flow. While no work brings 100 percent satisfaction, those who are purposeful about aligning what they do best to a particular need in the world are the most satisfied. The asset of doing engaging work represents approximately 40 percent of overall career satisfaction and effectiveness. In other words, if the nature of your work is not fulfilling, it is likely your Career Equity feels diminished.

How did you score on the Finding and Doing Engaging Work Assessment in Chapter 1?

Research indicates that those who achieve 35 points or more (or approximately 70 percent favorable responses) realize three interrelated career benefits. First, they report being happy or satisfied at work. Second, since they are more satisfied, they attract more and different opportunities. This is the "self-fulfilling" component of engaging work. The more you do engaging work, the more you gain. Third, those who do engaging work are more likely to stay in their role or with their firm. This retention results in a greater continuous career experience. Instead of moving from job to job every six months, those who cultivate engaging work realize the reward of seeing their work through to completion. Paradoxically, career persistence produces greater opportunities for career advancement. In other words, current and future employers recognize and desire people who stay engaged and achieve results. Engaging work translates into a higher probability of new career opportunities and career advancement.

If you feel you work hard but lack joy or fulfillment from your work, ask yourself three questions: Do I have a clear vision or definition of what engaging work means? Is there a high degree of fit or congruence between my unique skills and capabilities and the work I do? Finally, do I have an appreciative audience or people who value the contributions I make? The next section offers solutions and tools to help you find answers.

Creating A Clear Career Vision Of Engaging Work

"There is more to us than we know. If we can be made to see it, perhaps for the rest of our lives, we will be unwilling to settle for less."

—Kurt Hahn

The most important aspect of achieving great results, in any context, begins with clarity of what we want to achieve. This is especially relevant for building Career Equity. Much has been written about the importance of a vision or definition of an ideal future. Yet, despite the number of articles and books on this topic, research reveals fewer than 20 percent of professionals have clearly articulated what matters most to them. What is your ideal career? What do you want to be doing five years from now?

Without a vision or long-term goals, we run the risk of expending time, energy, and talent without realizing a feeling of success. Have you ever tried to complete a puzzle without a picture on the box? While some find it mentally challenging, most people become frustrated and quit. Creating a vision is a picture of a personal ideal. It guides our choices and increases belief in our ability to achieve what matters most. We know from research in personal and organizational development

21

that thinking and writing a vision increases the probability of achieving it.

A perfect example of a Career Equity builder and one who knows the power of a vision is Joe Cirulli. Joe's story, "The Believer," appeared in the August 2008 issue of *Inc.* magazine.

Joe is the CEO of three fitness clubs and four rehabilitation centers in Gainesville, Florida. His vision is to "keep Gainesville the healthiest city in America – one person, one business, one child at a time." He and his organization are well on their way to achieving this goal. Joe's inspiration came from reading one of my all-time favorite books, *Think and Grow Rich* by Napoleon Hill. From this book, Joe learned that the secret to success is in knowing what you want.

Joe took the time to write down 10 goals for his life. Most importantly, as Napoleon Hill recommends, Joe reviewed the list every morning and every night for the next few years. Notice, I did not say days, weeks, or months, but years! It is the mental rehearsal of aspirations that seem too big and too far away that turns them into reality.

Joe's vision included 10 key aspirations:
1) Own a health club in Gainesville.
2) Make it respected in the community.
3) Earn $100K by the age of 25.
4) Own a Mercedes-Benz, like the one driven by the Six Million Dollar Man.

5) Own a home in the mountains, another one near the ocean, and build a home for his parents.

6) Become a black belt in karate.

7) Become a pilot and own a plane.

8) Travel all over the United States.

9) Travel throughout the world.

10) Save $1 million.

It did take Joe over 10 years, but he has accomplished every one of the goals on his list and more. What is your career vision? Joe envisioned what career success meant to him in very specific terms and then acted in a systematic way to achieve them. Joe's path was not free from challenges or barriers. But in the process of pursuing his goals, Joe mastered an additional skill that enables Career Equity builders to create more of the engaging work they desire. That skill is the ability to suspend disbelief.

To fully realize your career potential and find the work most engaging, you must quiet the little voice inside that whispers or at times shouts "you can't do that."

Suspending Disbelief

One of my favorite quotes about the correlation between belief and achievement is by the founder of Ford Motor Company. Henry Ford built one of the largest companies in the world from nothing. He was quoted as saying "whether you think you can or you can't, you are usually right." The value of a vision is best observed in reverse or by looking backward. When we are setting out or beginning a new career, the prospect of achieving our vision may seem dim. It is the ability to suspend this disbelief that enables us to act and move forward. One of my best clients calls this act – faith. The difference between those who do engaging work and those who do not is determined by their belief in the ability to see the unknown. One tool for developing your vision and counteracting disbelief is called the Three-Year Letter. The value of this tool came home to me in a poignant way when a client and friend died unexpectedly. Jim was a true professional, among the top five percent of all financial services representatives.

Jim believed in the power of setting long-term goals for his career and life. Jim achieved significant results because he had a clear picture of career success and the ability to suspend disbelief. Jim was also a quiet leader. He was not one to shout his goals out publicly, but rather he reflected on what he wanted and acted with purpose to achieve it. After his funeral, his son, who is one of the top managing partners in Northwestern Mutual, and I were discussing Jim's approach to life. Matt mentioned that going through Jim's papers, the family found a "Three-Year Letter" Jim had written several years before. Matt was delighted that many of the aspirations his father defined were achieved. While we never know the time we are given, we can use our time and talent in the highest and best way, like Jim, by defining and acting on our vision.

Career Equity Tool: Three-Year Letter

While it is possible to define a Career Vision for the next five or 10 years, most professionals find three years to be a good place to begin. In a dynamic world where the rate of change is rapid and innovation is disrupting traditional organizations and business models, it is difficult for many people to imagine beyond three years. The key is to define the type of work that is engaging to you as specifically and clearly as you can. The more specific you are, the more likely you are to achieve your desired results.

Write your vision or letter in the present tense – seeing, feeling, and believing that the aspirations are achieved. In other words, write the letter assuming you have achieved success. After you write your letter make a promise to review it every few months and share it with a mentor or career advisor to increase your accountability. I strongly recommend reading the story on page 114 about how Zundra, Gail, and Sarajeni implemented a monthly review of their Three-Year Letters and achieved amazing results.

The Three-Year Letter template on the next page will get you started.

Dear (insert your name or someone important to you),
It is now (fill in date three years from today), I have achieved
a number of the aspirations I defined in (fill in today's date).
When I wrote this letter three years ago, I wondered if these
goals were really possible. Today, I can see how my
commitment, hard work, and courage to define my goals in
specific ways contributed to my success. The work I am doing
is engaging and interesting. Specifically, I enjoy_____
_____

The people who have most helped me achieve these career
goals are_____
Continuous learning and growth were essential to advancing
my career and making it more satisfying. Some of the learning
opportunities I pursued were   _____
_____

The most beneficial and rewarding lesson was_____
_____

Giving back to others was a key element of my plan. I believe
in the principle – give first and generously. For example, I
contributed_____

I am reaping great rewards for my hard work and dedication to
my goals and helping others succeed. My income is now

_____

_____

The recognition I received that matters most to me is _____

_____

_____

Today, thousands of Career Equity advocates have developed a Three-Year Letter. Do not be dismayed or frustrated if all your aspirations do not immediately come to mind. This is a process of self-discovery. Some professionals prefer to outline their aspirations with bullet points, others prefer a more creative approach with photos or images to represent their desired future. Use whatever format works for you. The important thing is to have something that defines where you are going.

Career Equity Builder Example

Finally, I want to close this chapter with a great example of a leader who was undeterred in pursuing his vision and how that persistence paid off. What will you learn from his story to help you achieve your career goals?

Corey graduated from De Smet Jesuit High School, a learning institution founded on the values of St. Ignatius of Loyola. After completing college at Miami University in Oxford, Ohio, with a degree in Philosophy in case he ever decided to become a Jesuit, Corey's first full-time career experience was selling medical equipment in the Pacific Northwest. It did not take him long to realize that this was not a fit for him. After two years, he returned to St. Louis without really knowing where his career or life was going.

One day, Fr. Chris Pinne, a Jesuit priest, phoned Corey. All he said was, "I like pizza." Corey said, "Okay Padre, I like pizza, too." The next day, Fr. Pinne drove 230 miles from Kansas City to St. Louis. He took Corey out for pizza. Corey says that Fr. Pinne more or less told him that he was making a mess of his life. But, like all good Jesuits, his dose of reality was tempered by a good measure of compassion: he invited Corey to apply for a job as an ASC (Alum Service Corps) volunteer teacher. Fr. Pinne, as Corey recalls, kept him on a short leash. He placed him at Rockhurst High School, a Jesuit school in Kansas City. It was at Rockhurst that Corey fell in love – with teaching, coaching, Ignatian spirituality and the Assistant Admissions Director; his now wife, Amanda.

As a first-year teacher at Rockhurst, Corey and a team of students and teachers made a trip to St. Louis to clear out the space that would eventually become home to De La Salle Middle School. This field trip would play a significant role in Corey's career and mission and underscores the importance that community contributions can make in our career growth.

After six years at Rockhurst, Corey had the opportunity to return to his alma mater, De Smet Jesuit High School in St. Louis, as a teacher. It was at De Smet where Corey developed clarity about his vision and passion for leading others. Corey recalls, "I felt privileged to share in a community where every person's gifts were celebrated and yet all were called to a higher level of service to our world."

This inspiration began to shape Corey's vision of more fully leading and living a core value of "Commitment to Doing Justice." Corey would recall his field trip to De La Salle Middle School, some 10 years earlier, as he learned about the opportunity to become the President of De La Salle. De La

Salle also has a strong faith foundation; it was founded by the Christian Brothers, who have been serving youth through the ministry of education since 1680.

During the interview, one of the Christian Brothers asked Corey to share his vision. Corey remembers clearly and confidently sharing – "to be the President or Principal of a Jesuit High School." No doubt his honesty and clarity impressed the Christian Brothers and they selected Corey to lead De La Salle Middle School through a formative time in its development.

For seven years, Corey helped De La Salle grow and thrive. The school doubled its annual fundraising revenue under Corey's leadership, went from having 30 days of cash in reserve to nearly one year's worth, and began the transition to a charter school with the aim of doubling the number of students served by the mission.

Then in late 2013, Corey's dream position opened. DeSmet Jesuit High School initiated a national search for a new Principal. After several months of interviewing and anticipation, Corey learned that someone else was selected for the role that he was so passionate to achieve. Imagine his disappointment. True to Corey's values, he accepted a lunch invitation from his previous competitor and congratulated him on his new role. Corey shared his original vision, and much to Corey's surprise, the new Principal told him that the current President was retiring and a search would be getting underway for the top spot. The former competitor encouraged Corey's career aspiration.

Like most Career Equity builders, Corey reached out to a long-time mentor for feedback on putting his name in the process a second time. Corey's mentor reminded him of his bigger vision and provided great feedback on how to communicate his intention for this role. On July 1st, Corey took the helm as DeSmet Jesuit High School's first lay President. Nearly twenty years after his original vision, he will have the opportunity to lead the learning and development of young men in the values that shaped his life and continue the legacy of "becoming a man for others," a core principle of St. Ignatius.

There are so many great career equity moments in Corey's story. From self-awareness and clarity of vision, to listening to mentors and career advocates, humility, and most importantly, faith. Oh, did I mention while working full-time at De La Salle that Corey set about completing his doctorate in Catholic School Leadership to enhance his learning and growth, and equip him with the academic credentials needed to lead a Jesuit learning institution? I hope Corey's story will inspire you to reconnect to your long-term aspirations and develop a plan to achieve them.

Fit Or Congruence Between Skills, Passion, And Work

"Where the needs of the world and your unique talents intersect is where you find your calling."

—Aristotle

In the international best seller *Good to Great*, author Jim Collins identifies that the most successful organizations or "great companies" do something good companies do not. They focus their time, talent, and resources on one thing they can do "best in the world." They do not try to be everything to everyone. The same principles apply to doing engaging work. Knowing what you are or can be best at in the world is the foundation of engaging work. What are, as Aristotle asks, your unique talents? Do you possess the skill or ability for photography, architectural design, or accounting? What are you passionate about contributing? What have others told you about your gifts or natural abilities? Consider John's story...

John knows great career advice can come anytime, anywhere. That is why when he found himself sitting next to the son-in-law of the chairman of RubinBrown, LLP at a wedding reception, he took advantage of the opportunity to listen.

John has a unique skill set. He is passionate about economics and predictive analytics, and believed this could be of value to RubinBrown's middle market clients. Based on a recommendation, chairman Jim Castellano met with John and came to a similar conclusion. He recommended that John meet with Michael Lewis, the partner in charge of Business Advisory Services. Business Advisory Services contains a highly effective Litigation Support group which helps clients with legal issues involving accounting malpractice, breaches, franchise/distributor disputes, intellectual property, lost profit quantification, product liability claims, and more.

Michael assigned John to one of the firm's high profile litigation cases. John's interest in sophisticated strategic analysis and performing complex calculations on large litigation and valuation projects were a perfect fit. John also learned that he thrives under the pressure that often accompanies these cases.

John's work was gaining greater visibility within the firm and externally. In fact, his work on his first big case enabled him to work closely with the Chairman who provided expert testimony. Because of his valuable skill set, John received multiple offers to join other large firms and technology companies as a data scientist. Many professionals would see this as an opportunity to cash in their career equity. True to John's skill set, he was more strategic. He recognized that his roots in St. Louis, strong relationships at RubinBrown, and most importantly, the sincere interest of senior leaders, were of great value to him. When John presented the chairman, managing partner, and leader of Business Advisory Group with a business plan about how to establish a new practice area in data-driven analytics, they listened.

Like most high-performing professionals, John likes to be continuously challenged. "I operate in a continuous state of discontent. However, the leaders I work with at RubinBrown are always willing to engage in conversation and challenge me. I can be very open with leaders at our firm and appreciate the access to the top decision makers."

John is having a great time building the business plan for the new practice. One year after his initial presentation to the partners, the team has completed their first data driven audit and has started to embed data-driven solutions across the firm.

"We are learning and modeling the impact of this new approach for other clients."

I asked John what he has learned through the process that could help others. He had four excellent Career Equity building strategies to offer:

1. Find the thing you are most interested in and commit to it. It is easy to get frustrated and walk away. However, success is never handed to you. No one is going to do it for you.

2. Find a firm that is committed to making an investment in your professional growth and provides open access to leaders like RubinBrown did for me.

3. Prove yourself. Working for one of the tech giants will provide you with a lot of resources, but it is a very structured career experience.

4. Take initiative for your growth and development.

If you are not as clear as John currently about your passion or plan, consider the Career Congruence Tool on Page 35. It can help you identify unique skills and passions in your past. Start with your first job. Did you babysit, cut lawns, or wait tables? Wherever your career journey began, make a list of all the things you enjoyed about this work in one column and then all of the things you disliked about the work or role in a second column. Repeat this for every job. Be specific. There are many tasks and activities in every position. Make sure that you capture those things that you enjoyed the most, were best at doing, and list them in priority order.

As you outline your career experiences, you will begin to see patterns and themes. For example, you may see a theme about working with people in a helping or service capacity. Or perhaps solving problems or selling concepts are common elements in the work you have found most engaging.

Ask yourself, how can I do more of the work that I enjoy? If you see a pattern or theme that does not appear in your current role or work do not be alarmed and certainly don't abandon your work – yet. In my experience, "The grass is greenest where it is watered." In other words, there may be a number of career opportunities awaiting you in your current organization or role that need to be more fully developed.

Bob's story is a great example of how a long-held passion and interest can become a meaningful career with work and intention. Bob grew up volunteering for the Special Olympics of Kansas to support his brother who had a mental disability. Like many Career Equity builders, Bob discovered the mutual satisfaction that comes from helping others in need. He played soccer for the Kansas Olympic development team and played for four years in college at Drury University while earning his Bachelor's degree in Education.

Bob has a passion for outdoor and adventure sports. He loves camping, canoeing, mountain biking, skiing, snowboarding, hiking and trail running. After college, Bob's career aspiration changed. Instead of a formal teaching position, Bob pursued

CAREER CONGRUENCE TOOL	Type of work	What I enjoyed about this work:	What I disliked about this work:
First Job			
Second Job			
Third Job			
Etc.			

various sales roles that gave him the flexibility to enjoy his many outdoor avocations in his off hours. Ultimately, he enjoyed working in the independent food service sales industry for more than 16 years. One day Bob gained a new food service account with Cedar Lake Cellars. Cedar Lake Cellars is a privately held business in the heart of Missouri Wine Country. The Winery, restaurant, and event venues sit on more than 170 scenic acres. The Cedar Lake property also contains a unique facility for mud runs, an event where participants negotiate an obstacle course many of which are filled with water and mud, called The Battlegrounds.

Bob was introduced to the race director of The Battlegrounds. "I had not heard about mud runs but thought it sounded like a great way to blend my passion for the outdoors and physical fitness in a scenic setting. I wanted to get involved and learn more about this new industry crossing the nation." Bob offered to volunteer at The Battlegrounds to learn more about the runs and build relationships for future food service opportunities. Bob's initiative landed him the role of "Volunteer Coordinator" for a race in June. Bob's sales experience, ability to work well with people and passion for outdoor adventures enabled him to be very effective at this role. He recruited more than 125 volunteers. The following year, Bob continued his work in foodservice sales and built his reputation with the Cedar Lake and Battlegrounds owner and team. Intentional development of knowledge and relationships always sets someone up for a win.

When the Battlegrounds race director left, Bob recognized the opportunity to make a career change. He took the initiative to ask the owner of The Battlegrounds, Carl Bolm, about filling the gap due to the director's departure. The owner offered Bob a part-time position to learn the business and demonstrate results. Bob jumped in and proved himself by creating an in-depth marketing plan and standard operating procedures to make each race run more efficiently and effectively. About six months after Bob started in his role, The Battlegrounds had its biggest success to date. More than 1300 runners enjoyed the fun and engaging course and Bob's hard work and initiative earned him the full-time role of Director of The Battlegrounds. Now Bob has his sights set on doubling the runners for each race, every year. You can rest assured Bob will jump over or remove any obstacles in his way.

An Appreciative Audience

Another component of doing engaging work involves surrounding ourselves with people who can help us more fully recognize and act upon our unique talents. In her book *Necessary Dreams*, author and psychiatrist, Dr. Anna Fels, says "the wish for mastery is undoubtedly a key component of ambition and success. But the pursuit of mastery virtually always requires a specific context: an evaluating, encouraging audience must be present for skills and talents to develop."

Who is your appreciative audience? Who encourages you to try new things, and affirms your ideas or dreams? Recently, as part of work with an international accounting firm, I interviewed each member of a large engagement team. Our discussions focused on how the firm helped them achieve their career aspirations and what kept them energized and committed to the firm's goals. The responses of one staff person stood out to me. When I asked her what motivated her to stay with the firm, she pulled out a notecard from her portfolio. On it was a handwritten message from a partner who was her mentor. She told me that the previous year she was working on a big project for a very demanding client and deadlines were tight. "The partner took the time during this intense project to tell me how much he appreciated my commitment and dedication. It made me feel so important to the team and the firm." This

Note to firm leaders:

A handwritten note to members of your team during challenging projects is an antidote for turnover and supports team members' long-term aspirations.

staff person's work and dedication were noticed by leaders and, as a result, it increased her feeling of career engagement.

In my experience, the presence or lack of an appreciative audience correlates directly with the extent to which we describe our work as engaging. This element also links closely with the next chapter on cultivating meaningful relationships. The key point here is that our satisfaction or engagement is influenced by the people with whom we work. If we believe our co-workers and leaders care about us and appreciate our contributions, we will find work more engaging. Conversely, the lack of an appreciative audience often predicts dissatisfaction and ultimately departure.

Having an appreciative audience does not always mean getting positive feedback. Some of the best growth and learning comes from leaders who are willing to provide challenging feedback.

Telling the truth is a far greater gift, even when it is not easy; as this senior associate learned in his mid-year review:

"I have a lot to improve upon to achieve a promotion to manager. I wouldn't have known this if Steve did not take the time and have the courage to tell me what I didn't want to hear during my performance review. In reflecting on what he said, I had to agree with most of it. I wouldn't have gotten this out of my review if he was sugarcoating."

Those who possess a high degree of engaging work and Career Equity know they cannot wait passively for others to praise their work. If you want more you must give more. Recognition must be earned and reciprocal. Giving a high degree of energy, enthusiasm, and engagement on a project precedes appreciation. Finally, when was the last time you were an appreciative audience for your co-worker or even your boss? Reciprocating with genuine recognition to others not only strengthens work relationships, it increases our energy and satisfaction.

Doing engaging work is achieved by having a clear and compelling direction for your career future or vision. Ideally, your vision is written and reviewed frequently to help suspend the natural disbelief that may occur during your pursuit of bold goals.

Additionally, your clarity about your unique skills and capabilities increases the probability of doing work that utilizes those strengths.

Finally, engaging work depends on the people with whom we work. Co-workers, clients, or leaders provide feedback, enhance career growth and affirm our aspirations. With a clear vision, congruence between skills and work, and an appreciative audience, we accumulate the value of interesting work with less effort and more *flow*.

Extra Credit

1) Read "The Believer," Bo Birlingham, *Inc.* (August 1, 2008)
2) Read *Think and Grow Rich,* Napoleon Hill – especially Chapter 2, New York: The Random House Publishing Group, 1960.
3) Write your Three-Year Letter and share with a mentor or career advisor.

3: Cultivating Meaningful Relationships

"There is no such thing as a self-made person. You reach your goals only with the help of others."

—George Shinn

"I was ready for a new challenge and reached out to a woman business owner I admired for career guidance. During the breakfast meeting at her club, she pointed across the room to a business leader whom she knew was looking for a senior executive to help him grow his firm. She made a generous introduction about my skills and experience. Later that same day, he called me to schedule a time to meet and discuss the opportunity he was trying to fill. Three months later, I was fully employed in one of the most satisfying roles in my career. Without this connection and relationship, one of the best parts of my career would have never happened."

—Senior HR Professional at Boeing

This story is full of evidence about why meaningful relationships are one of the best predictors of career opportunity, satisfaction, and advancement. It points to the importance of taking the initiative to seek feedback from leaders we admire and being open to new career directions.

Who in your life shares ideas or resources that enable you to look at an issue from another perspective? Who do you know who cares enough to provide a great testimonial about your career accomplishments or offer challenging feedback about things you do not want to hear but need to hear?

Marcus Buckingham, author of the acclaimed *Now, Discover Your Strengths*, surveyed more than 20,000 professionals in diverse industries. His research reveals that the primary predictor of career satisfaction and effectiveness is not technology, training, or the company you work for. It is the quality of a relationship with a specific manager or leader.

The absence of meaningful relationships at work is costly. Exit interviews with more than 1,000 employees at a large international accounting firm revealed that a lack of a meaningful relationships makes turnover eight times more likely. Mark Granovetter's classic study, highlighted in *Getting a Job*, underscores the importance of relationships when pursuing new career opportunities. Granovetter researched employment histories of hundreds of professionals and technical workers in Boston. He discovered that 60 percent of those who found a new job went through a personal connection. A more contemporary perspective provided by Pam Lassiter, author of *The New Job Security*, highlights that networking can be daunting, particularly for those with more of an introverted personality. Lassiter encourages job seekers to do it anyway. "Using your networking wisely is a muscle you can exercise and develop if you haven't already. Outplacement and alumni career services surveys report that 65 to 85 percent of job seekers find their jobs through networking."

For all of these reasons and more, cultivating meaningful relationships is essential to building Career Equity.

Taking Stock Of Meaningful Relationships

Do you have the relationships you need to learn and grow in new directions?

Now is a good time to take stock of relationships that matter most to you in your professional life. Developing diverse and relevant relationships demands both attention and intention. Professionals who have deep Career Equity make relationship building a priority and take the initiative to keep relationships current. Social network theory tells us that the shape of a network determines its usefulness. Small, tighter networks are less useful than networks with multiple broader connections. More open networks introduce more new ideas and opportunities than closed networks with many redundant ties. In other words, a group of friends who only do things with each other share the same knowledge and opportunities. A group of individuals with connections to other social worlds have access to a wider range of information.

Clearly, we enjoy affiliating with people with whom we have common values and interests. However, when professional networks are limited to "people like me," they limit career growth. Who are the current relationships in your Career Equity portfolio? Use the Career Board of Directors

43

CAREER BOARD OF DIRECTORS TOOL

Name	Expertise	Organization and Role	Age	Gender	Race	Met last
Example: Rachel Smith		Partner at Smith and Burns	37	F	W	Dec. 2015

Tool on Page 44 to capture the names and characteristics of relationships most meaningful to you now.

What patterns and themes do you observe about your current "meaningful" relationships? How diverse are their backgrounds? How do your aspirations align with theirs? When was the last time that you let them know that they have made, and continue to make, a meaningful contribution to your career?

Who Is "On Board" With Your Career?

Knowing where you stand today with current relationships is a critical first step in cultivating meaningful relationships. If your assessment reveals a high degree of diversity in expertise, race, gender, age, and organizational level, you have a strong network that will serve you well. However, most professionals find their relationships are overrepresented in one industry, firm, age, race, and/or gender. This is an opportunity to expand relationship diversity. Just like an investment portfolio, diversity yields better results over the long-term.

When Kim was thinking of making a change in her career to corporate finance, she made a list of relationships in her network. Kim remembered that a regional leadership program she participated in gave her the opportunity to meet several finance professionals. Once Kim shared her plan with them, they were willing to introduce her to a Chief Financial Officer (CFO) in a company she was targeting. Kim was surprised that connections developed outside of her immediate organization were the catalyst to realizing her career goals.

In *Achieving Success through Social Capital,* author Wayne E. Baker reports that most Americans cultivate homogenous networks. Twenty percent of Americans talk with only one person about important matters. Some do not talk with anyone at all. In today's dynamic professional world, a small, homogeneous network does not provide adequate support nor optimize learning. Cultivating meaningful relationships is not about quantity. It is about diversity and quality. It is about raising our awareness and intention of the great relationships we possess and the courage to build new ones. One tool for increasing the quality and depth of meaningful career relationships is to think of these people as a Career Board of Directors.

The Career Board Of Directors: Advisors Who Help You Build Career Equity

"What every leader needs are advisors who will tell you the brutal truth even when it is something you don't want to hear."
—*Jimmy Carter, U.S. President*

Chief Executive Officers (CEOs) of public companies know the importance of diverse meaningful relationships. These people are often known as a "Board of Directors." Boards are a necessity for a public company or a non-profit organization. They ensure that the public good or shareholder interests are met. James Kristie, editor of the publication *Directors and Boards,* says, "A Board offers their intelligence, integrity, and courage to exercise dutiful oversight of management and contribute in meaningful ways to the strategic affairs of the enterprise. Without a thoughtful, engaged, and ethical conscience, the CEO can become distracted from her core purpose and put an organization, people, and personal careers in jeopardy."

Clearly, Boards steer the strategy and guide the success of an organization. How could this model benefit your career? Would a trusted group of individuals using their intelligence, integrity, and courage guide you to better results?

How do you build a Career Board of Directors? For some professionals, a Career Board is very structured. These professionals develop a formal process of inviting members to the Board, scheduling meetings, and reporting career goals and results. For others simply having this mental model adds substance to their career portfolio. The level of structure you choose for a Career Board is up to you.

However you proceed, thinking like the CEO of your career, will expand your perspective and open you to diverse feedback. Three guiding principles have helped hundreds of professionals build or enhance their Career Board of Directors.

1) Quality, not size matters. Do not build a Board with 15 people. It is best to build a Board with a small number of strong relationships. Look at your current relationships and select one or two advisors. Then add one or two new relationships to foster your growth outside of your "comfort zone." When

recruiting people to your Career Board, start by asking: Will they be able to dedicate time to help me? Highly visible business leaders are a great resource, but they may be too busy.

2) Do they demonstrate the ability and courage to be open and honest? Deep relationships and learning come from open, honest feedback. A group of "yes" people will not produce the growth you are seeking. Identify people who will challenge you to look at the things you want to avoid.

3) Do they have diverse perspectives, backgrounds, or experiences? As we have discussed earlier, diversity is an important dimension of career success. Seek it.

Take a moment to list advisors you want to cultivate:

❑ _____

❑ _____

❑ _____

❑ _____

Many professionals get stuck at this point. They are comfortable identifying people who can add value but uncomfortable taking these relationships to a deeper level. Asking people for guidance and time requires an emotional risk. Risk is a prerequisite to growth. I recommend taking Mike's lead in building out your Career Board of Directors. It is a great example of how with initiative and clarity we can all build new meaningful relationships. Mike was a director at one of the region's top accounting firms when he completed the Career Board of Director's Tool (see Page 44). Mike noticed that his Board lacked ethnic diversity. While this is not an uncommon observation for most professionals, Mike is Hispanic and takes great pride in his heritage and the diverse perspectives of others. Mike thought about those he admired in business and who would challenge him to think bigger and more strategically. The CEO of one of the fastest growing Fortune 100 companies in the United States came to mind and who also had a Hispanic background. Mike took the courageous step to ask the CEO to serve as one of his career advisors. He framed his request succinctly and let the CEO know it would not demand significant time; rather a few meetings a year to gain his insight and perspective.

To the CEO's credit he conducted a bit of due diligence himself. He asked Mike about his background and goals for their time together. Through his "fact finding," he discovered that they were both alumni of the accounting firm Coopers Lybrand and had similar Mexican heritage. The bottom line – the CEO agreed to serve as Mike's advisor. Mike mentioned to me that while he was initially apprehensive about approaching such a significant person he remembered that the worst-case scenario was that the CEO would decline his invitation, and he would be in the same position he was in before he asked. He had nothing to lose and a great deal to gain.

Who could help you get a bigger and broader perspective on your career goals? As the philosopher Johann Wolfgang von Goethe says "Whatever you can do or dream you can, begin it. Boldness has genius, power and magic in it!"

Mike's story is about moving quickly from thought to action. To help you reduce the space between knowing you need to do something differently and actually implementing it consider advice from Donna Fischer, author of *People Power: 12 Principles to Enrich Your Business, Career, and Personal Networks*.

Fischer shares two best practices for building new relationships. First, she says, be clear about what you want and how you think this person can help. For example, how often would you like to meet with them? Clarity of purpose helps others help you. Your career advisors will be more effective if they are clear about what you are trying to achieve. Organize and prepare for your meetings in advance. Do not waste an advisor's valuable time with unstructured meetings and vague objectives.

A best practice to follow is the approach recently used by the CFO of a $300 million dollar company. He called me to ask for feedback on how to increase his community involvement. He listed two or three criteria describing the type of organization he wanted to serve and the role he wanted to play. This type of pre-engagement creates a favorable impression and results in more specific actionable feedback.

Fischer's second suggestion is to tell potential advisors what is special about them and what caused you to ask for their help. This action step goes a long way toward cultivating meaningful relationships. Do you remember the last time someone asked you for help because of your special talents, knowledge, or gifts? How did you feel? People are flattered by a specific request. Even if they are too busy to serve as an advisor, they will respect you for asking.

A Career Equity Builder Example

"It was my fifth year as a financial advisor and I hit a wall. I was behind in my production goals, my assistant resigned, and my income was not sufficient to support my growing family. My first thought was to leave. Quit. Go back to a good job at Kodak as a sales manager. My managing partner knew I was struggling. He knew an outside perspective would increase the effectiveness of my decision making. He arranged a meeting with the firm's strategic business advisor. She gave me valuable feedback and strategies to help me persist during this difficult time. I also formed a "Board of Advisors" that was, and continues to be, an invaluable source of feedback and support. All of these relationships made a significant difference in my career decisions. I just celebrated my eleventh anniversary with the firm. I've achieved the industry's top sales award and will be opening my own district office this year. What is clear to me now is that without the mentoring and support from outside coaches and my advisory board, I would not have remained. I would have settled for something below my capabilities."

Fred's story perfectly illustrates the value of mentors and forming a Board of Advisors. Without feedback and support at a critical time, Fred may have made a different decision and not realized his full potential in his profession.

Three Steps To Cultivating More Meaningful Relationships

After you recruit trusted career advisors, you will want to focus on retaining these meaningful relationships. The following three steps outline how to keep important relationships mutually beneficial.

Step 1: Listen. Stephen Covey's bestselling book, *The Seven Habits of Highly Effective People,* highlights the habit of "seeking first to understand, and then be understood." It is a critical habit in developing interdependence and strong relationships. Many professionals express that it is an attribute of tremendous value but difficult to master. When you have identified the relationships you want to cultivate, make sure you listen closely to your selected advisors. Ask questions about their background, experiences, and lessons learned. Engage them by asking follow-up questions and taking note of their responses. You identified these individuals because of their skills, expertise, and unique perspective. Make sure you gain as much as you can by listening and learning from their experiences.

Step 2: Ask and Act. Planning and analyzing are critical components of building Career Equity. However, *action* drives results. Many successful business executives believe that an idea 20 percent planned and 80 percent executed is superior to an idea 80 percent planned and 20 percent executed. Ask for feedback and input from your trusted career advisors and then *act.* People will be more likely to contribute to your career growth if they see that you act on their guidance.

In addition, integrate your planning and acting by establishing a Career Advisor Connection Calendar. Planning ahead to meet with advisors and keeping them informed of your accomplishments produces great results. Few business professionals want to be a career crisis counselor. Be proactive and stay in touch when things are going well, too.

Step 3: Acknowledge Contributions. When I was young, my mother taught me to send a thank you note within a few days of receiving a gift. A handwritten note of thanks, not an e-mail, is an expression people treasure. When someone gives you their time and attention, it is a gift. Be sure you honor this with an expression of appreciation.

Jon Magin is a great example of a Career Equity builder who used the three steps to cultivate relationships that have had a meaningful impact on his long-term career direction. Today, Jon is a manager at West Monroe Partners, a consulting firm that has fully integrated Career Equity into all firm people practices. Jon joined West Monroe Partners in 2007, right out of college. The Seattle office was just getting underway and Jon was one of the firm's first consultants. Jon loves his work but like many consultants the travel demands were significant and began to interfere with some of Jon's personal aspirations. Jon attended a Career Equity learning session I facilitated in the Seattle office. After training, Jon completed his Three-Year Letter where he articulated a desire to spend less time traveling in his career future.

Shortly after training, Jon was staffed on a local client in Seattle. Jon thought this was a great fit for his career as it required no travel and fully utilized his skills. Jon did such a great job on the project the client offered Jon a full-time position. While this was a wonderful recognition of his contribution to their business, Jon struggled with the decision. He loved WMP and envisioned becoming a senior manager or partner. However, the new client opportunity was with a great organization, involved a significant increase in pay and required no travel. Jon needed a strategy to make this pivotal career choice. Utilizing the five Career Equity assets as a framework, Jon evaluated each opportunity against engaging work, meaningful relationships, learning and growth, contributing to community and culture, and the right rewards and recognition. Engaging work, meaningful relationships, and rewards and recognition were all superior at West Monroe. But the work, travel and rewards (pay) at the new opportunity were great, too. Jon realized that he needed feedback from trusted advisors to gain some objectivity and perspective. He contacted several of his Career Board of Directors. Among Jon's advisors were a consultant who went to industry and loved it, a business leader who was in industry but had never been a consultant, and one of his WMP managers, Kent. Kent is a "players' coach" and sophisticated manager. Jon said "Kent appreciated that I came to him. We have a high trust relationship and I could be transparent with him. He also is a great listener and was very objective. He was concerned about helping me make the right decision, not selling WMP. Kent helped me realize that it was not just about the money and that one of the most important aspects of my work satisfaction is developing and teaching others." The opportunity offered by the client was an independent contributor role that did not provide an opportunity for Jon to develop or mentor others. What career path did Jon choose? Jon has now accumulated more than eight years of Career Equity at West Monroe Partners, a unique milestone in the consulting industry. "The Career Equity framework and the meaningful relationships on my Career Board helped me make a great decision during a difficult situation," Jon said.

Career Equity Builder Example

Each year, thousands of students graduate from college and begin the process of converting formal education into engaging and meaningful work. One of the best ways to accelerate this process is to form a Career Board of Directors to guide their job search. Vanessa's story is a great example of how cultivating existing relationships can unlock opportunities that before seemed remote. Vanessa dreamed of transforming urban environments by using her talents and interests in architecture, design, and organizational development to shape the built environment into a more effective community. She was eager to gain opportunities in urban development or consulting firms that specialized in urban renewal projects. However, Vanessa felt she lacked the relationships necessary to open the desired doors. She had been applying to numerous online positions but was not getting beyond her initial response to the posting. We discussed how a Career Board could help her increase the probability of finding opportunities rarely posted publicly. More importantly, it could offer new strategies for reaching decision makers. With a little structure and intentional thinking, Vanessa was able to identify professionals from her former internship assignments and friends that she had initially overlooked. For example, her best friend's father was the head of an architecture and design firm specializing in urban renewal projects. This asset was simply waiting for Vanessa to activate it.

After creating a list of five to six people that represented a diverse group of professionals Vanessa admired, she set up meetings and phone conferences with each individual. She shared why she thought of them as a member of her Career Board of Directors and asked if she could seek their feedback throughout her search process. Here are a few of Vanessa's directors:

- HR Consultant specializing in helping employers find the right talent for their organization

- President of an Architecture and Design Firm, specializing in Urban Planning

- Former boss from an urban planning internship

- Associate project manager at McCormack Baron Salazar, a global leader in real estate consulting.

What percent of the people Vanessa asked accepted the opportunity to help her? Correct – 100 percent. Most people are delighted to be asked and are eager to help, especially when the process is well organized and managed. Most importantly, Vanessa did not sit back and wait for people to bring her opportunities. She provided her directors with updates on her search activity and sought feedback about potential next actions. I encourage career seekers to update directors every other week via a brief email. This discipline shows the Board that you are serious and persistent in pursuing important goals. Both behaviors build trust and confidence in relationships and the willingness of others to help you achieve your goals. I am often asked for practical examples of how people engage their directors. Here is an excerpt from one of Vanessa's updates that is very well done:

Dear Board Members,

I hope you are having a nice week. I just wanted to update you on a few things about my job search.

- *I am in the process of applying for a job at TDC in Boston. They provide research and consulting in the non-profit sector and I found the position through the Vanderbilt Career website. They require references and I was wondering if I could list your name as a reference? I am also asking my former boss and reconnecting with him about possible opportunities in Saint Louis.*

- *I have talked to Patience and Emily and they are willing to connect me with additional people as well. I just need to book a time to come home soon.*

- *I sent in my information to Development Strategies and Emily also forwarded my information to her contact there (she is willing to do this for all of the Saint Louis applications for whom she has contacts, which is terrific). Today I am also going to reach out to a contact there that Mr. Smith gave me to make sure my information was received and to gather more information about openings (they just had a general HR address where you send you cover letter and resume too, but not a specific job).*

- *I am in the process of applying to a Community Support Representative position at Wells Fargo in Bethesda, MD.*

- *Later this week I will start an application to the Saint Louis Regional Chamber (Emily mentioned she had contacts there as well).*

- *My goals for this week are to finalize travel plans and finish the three applications: TDC, Wells Fargo, and the St. Louis Regional Chamber. Then I will send out updates to my career board. Thank you so much for all your help and guidance!*

Can you see how clear, concise, and accountable Vanessa is with her communication? Do you notice how Board members helped her make connections she would not have had without them? Further Vanessa was working on multiple directions and opportunities concurrently. She did not wait passively. She took initiative and did an excellent job of following up with urgency. The end result of this intentional effort? Vanessa realized her aspiration of using her diverse skills in planning, community and organizational development and started her career immediately following graduation as the Director of Research at Development Strategies, Inc.

In summary, building a diverse Career Board of Directors will accelerate your career growth. Acting on your Directors' feedback and acknowledging their contributions will build more meaningful relationships and equip you with an essential component of Career Equity.

Career Growth By Helping Others Succeed

"It is one of the most beautiful compensations of this life that no one can sincerely try to help another without helping himself."

—*Ralph Waldo Emerson*

One of the most powerful ways to cement learning and continue growing meaningful relationships is to teach others what you have learned. Sharing your knowledge reflects a principle of stewardship. Webster defines *stewardship* as: *"Conducting, supervising, or managing something; especially the careful and responsible management of something entrusted to one's care."*

Serving as a trusted career advisor for someone else is an act of stewardship that builds your skills and capacity to lead and develop others. Mike, Chief Operating Officer of a growing company, is responsible for growing and expanding four business units, and knows the mutual value of helping others succeed.

More than 20 years ago, Mike benefited from the patient coaching and guidance of a senior engineer named Jack. Mike says his meeting with Jack is as vivid today as if it were yesterday.

"I was a new hire in engineering at Pfizer and was asked to replace a distillation column. I had no idea what a distillation column was. I went to Jack and admitted my shortcoming and braced myself for the standard, "Didn't they teach you that in college?" Instead, Jack invited me into his office and spent more than 30 minutes creating detailed drawings and explaining the function of a distillation column and how to replace it. Jack did not show off his knowledge. He truly cared about helping me."

Today, when one of Mike's protégés approaches him with what seems like a fundamental question, he remembers Jack's mentoring. He is careful not to dismiss their questions but takes the time to listen and teach them how to succeed. Take a moment and reflect on protégés, colleagues, or family members who would benefit from developing their own Career Board. Who comes to mind? If you mentor more than one person, you may want to consider bringing your protégés together in a Mentoring Circle. Mentoring Circles function like book clubs or discussion groups. Each month a member brings a topic for the group to read about and discuss.

At your next team meeting, you could discuss the concepts in this chapter and ask members to consider the relationships that are guiding their career. Is it time to schedule a Career Equity conversation with one of your best professionals? If your current role includes managing or developing others, you will want to read Chapter 8. There is nothing more motivating and effective than showing interest in an individual's personal career goals.

What happens when you give unconditionally to others? You reap rewards that provide opportunities you could not have imagined. Susan's story exemplifies how doing what you love and being open to helping others opens new doors. Susan Conrad is a leader with a passion for building personal relationships and helping leaders increase the value of their organization. Susan has a strong background in business and finance, both experientially and academically. She earned a Bachelor's degree in Finance from the University of Missouri and a Masters of Business Administration (MBA) from Washington University. After playing a leadership role in a family business, Susan started her own commercial real estate management and consulting firm.

Susan helped St. Louis companies boost the value of their real estate in significant ways for nearly 15 years, and these real estate business engagements often expanded to other consultative engagements with her clients. For example, when Moneta Group purchased its 78,000-square-foot headquarters building, Conrad helped the financial consulting firm completely remodel the building's interior and renew and expand other tenants' leases – what Conrad refers to as "back of the house" work, including asset management. With Susan's help, Moneta was able to boost the value of its corporate headquarters by more than 25 percent.

My relationship with Susan began several years ago, when she was on the Board of Directors of a non-profit organization dedicated to breaking the cycle of poverty by providing exceptional educational opportunities for young women (another testament to her Career Equity in community involvement). Susan is a Career Equity champion. She believes in the concepts and generously gives her time to helping others who are working through a career transition or in need of feedback on their professional growth.

Therefore, it was really fun when Susan approached me with a desire to use the Career Equity tools to guide her own career transition. She had built a successful firm and was ready for a new challenge. We started by expanding her Career Board of Directors and meeting on a monthly basis to help her organize a plan to investigate new possibilities. Implementing Career Equity principles always demands initiative and discipline but making a change from a successful business to an unknown opportunity is especially challenging. Most professionals make a change when an existing experience ends, when they are feeling dissatisfied with a current role or organization, or someone approaches them with a new prospect. Moving from something successful, established and profitable to a new role in an undefined organization requires a healthy dose of self-motivation, persistence, and faith.

Over a 14-month process, Susan met with nearly 30 people. Learning about roles and opportunities she would never have imagined was stimulating. She also had to learn to say "no" to things that were good opportunities, but not great ones. Because of Susan's established track record of professional performance, strong relationships, relentless pursuit of learning, community giving, and financial success, she received numerous offers. To select the best opportunity meant resisting the temptation to settle for something that did not align with all of her aspirations and reasons for making the change in the first place. In the end, Susan's prior work and relationships brought her full-circle to one of her former clients, mentioned earlier in the story, the Moneta Group. Today, Susan is the Chief Strategy and Human Resources Officer for the firm. This is a perfect fit for Susan. She is an intentional relationship builder working in a comprehensive planning firm whose long-term success is dependent on building trusted relationships internally and externally. She is a critical member of the leadership team and trusted business advisor to the firm's 39 partners regarding the firm's vision, culture, and plans for growth. Additionally, through her work as the firm's People leader, she is helping Moneta professionals build their Career Equity and develop future leaders for Moneta's long-term sustainability. When asked what she would tell others contemplating this type of career change, Susan shared "Don't be afraid to dream big and ask for help."

Extra Credit

1) Read *People Power: 12 Power Principles to Enrich your Business, Career, & Personal Networks,* Donna Fischer (Austin, TX: Bard Press, 1995).

2) Read *The Tipping Point: How Little Things Can Make A Big Difference,* Malcolm Gladwell (New York: Little, Brown and Company, 2000).

3) Form a Mentoring Circle of newer professionals and discuss how they are managing their relationships.

4: Relentlessly Pursuing Learning and Growth

"A mind stretched to a new idea never goes back to its original dimensions."

—*Oliver Wendell Holmes*

"I have always been passionate about learning new things, but Australia was never part of my career plan. It turned out to be one of the best experiences of my life." This insight comes from Kathy, a certified public accountant (CPA) in a firm that offers international exchange opportunities to its best professionals.

Firm leaders invited Kathy to be part of an audit team in Sydney, Australia, when she was beginning her third year on the audit staff. The assignment required a six-month commitment. She knew an experience in another country would give her unique learning and growth opportunities – differentiating her from other professionals. When Kathy returned from Australia, firm leaders were eager to hear what lessons she had learned. The managing partner asked Kathy to share her experiences with all firm members at the Annual Meeting and create a You-Tube video to share with potential recruits.

Kathy's experience is a great example of the five learning catalysts Career Equity builders use to relentlessly learn and grow. In this chapter, we will describe each of the five learning catalysts and offer best practices to accelerate learning assets.

Catalyst 1: Be Open To New Opportunities

Kathy would not have realized exponential growth in technical, interpersonal, and leadership skills without being open to a new opportunity. While an international assignment sounds intriguing, it demands significant change in familiar schedules, work locations, relationships, and conveniences. Consider that Australia is on a different continent and 15 hours ahead of the time when Kathy's family and friends are awake and working. Just calling a friend demands a new lexicon of international phone codes and mental gymnastics. Career Equity builders embrace new opportunities and seek situations that get them out of their "comfort zone." They exemplify Eleanor Roosevelt's wisdom: "Do one thing everyday that scares you."

cat·a·lyst [kátt'list] n.
stimulus to change:
somebody or something that makes a change happen or brings about an event

However, you do not need to travel halfway around the world to embrace new learning and growth. In fact, new opportunities beckon us constantly. The key is to be aware of them and say yes to them when they are right for you. For example, when was last time you were aware of a business meeting like a local business journal breakfast seminar or video conference on a new technical skill? Did you take advantage of the opportunity or persist with your familiar routine? Opportunities abound if we are paying attention. A few years ago, I was in my friend Anne's office. Anne is a bank executive and her clients are business owners and CEOs. I noticed a brochure on her desk of a beautiful mountain ranch home. She told me "Last Chance Ranch" was in Aspen, Colorado, and belonged to the CEO of a well-known company that had a strong relationship with the bank. She thought I would enjoy meeting him because he was very intent on building a values-driven organization and developing leaders.

Several weeks later, Anne created the opportunity for me to meet the CEO and the leader of his organizational change practice. Over the next year, the three of us met several times to discuss leadership and organizational-growth strategies. Eighteen months after seeing the brochure, I was invited to facilitate a discussion with six other CEOs on leadership development at the Aspen retreat I originally admired. How are you attending to the things that energize and inspire you? How might a conversation open a door to a new learning or insight?

Catalyst 2: Participate In Professionals Associations

Are you a member of a nationally recognized professional association? If you are, how would you describe your level of engagement or contribution? If you are like most professionals, you pay your annual dues and toss the complimentary magazine in the "read later" pile. Professional memberships are often an underutilized Career Equity asset. Consider the following ways professional affiliations can build equity with a reasonable level of effort and intention:

1) Provide the latest technical or industry knowledge in magazines, websites, journals, etc.

2) Increase the depth and breadth of your professional network, including access to senior leadership in your profession.

3) Offer a forum to increase your professional "brand" through speaking or writing opportunities.

4) Develop leadership skills by choosing to serve on a committee, task force, or in an officer role.

As we know from Chapter 1, Tasha discovered that involvement in a professional association opened new doors to career opportunities. She took the initiative to find the local chapter of the Society of Human Resource Management Association (HRMA) and did not stop there. She researched the intern program and after several months of showing up and being a contributor, she contacted me at Arthur Andersen, where in my role at the firm I was an active member of HRMA. Because Tasha invested time and energy in the Association, she gained awareness of new opportunities and access to decision makers that she would not have without active involvement.

Catalyst 3: Mentoring

Mentoring has been around for centuries. In fact, we get the term *mentor* from Greek mythology. When Odysseus left for the Trojan War, he placed Mentor in charge of his palace and his son, Telemachus, to guide development of this future king. Gaining a mentor is a highly efficient and effective learning and growth strategy. One mentoring meeting can yield numerous benefits. For example, a mentor can help you gain new technical knowledge, role play how to deliver challenging feedback to a team member, bolster your self-confidence, or help you think more strategically about long-term career opportunities. In today's business world, mentors possess experience, expertise, or wisdom and a willingness to share this with another, typically less experienced, professional. The Mentor Hall of Fame (www.mentors.ca) compiled by Rey Carr includes examples of great business leaders and the mentoring advice they gained. The following are a few excerpts from Carr's list:

- Herb Kelleher (Founder and chairman of Southwest Airlines) was mentored by his mother Ruth, who told him, "Respect people for who they are, not for what their titles are."

- Benjamin Graham (Columbia University professor) and Howard Buffett (dad), mentors to Warren Buffett (CEO, Berkshire Hathaway), told him, "You're right not because others agree with you, but because your facts are right."

- Warren Bennis, mentor to Howard Schultz (CEO, Starbucks), suggested to his mentee, "Recognize the skills and traits you don't possess, and hire the people who have them."

Who are your mentors? What characteristics or attributes do they possess that are of value to you? What guidance have they given? As a Career Equity builder, it is unlikely you have arrived at this point without a mentor. These meaningful relationships are an essential asset. As a learning and growth strategy, they are a source of rich information and feedback that peers may not have the courage or inclination to share. How often are you soliciting mentor time and feedback? Do you prepare for these meetings to ensure that you are getting the most from their wisdom? What do you do after the meeting to ensure new learning or insights are acted on? We often think of mentoring as benefitting the protégés. However, research reveals that the mentor gains as much, if not more, from a mentoring experience than the understudy. As you begin to realize benefits from several mentors, begin to think how you could learn and grow from mentoring others.

Catalyst 4: Cultivate Reading Rituals

"Those who cannot remember the past are condemned to repeat it."

—*George Santayana, Spanish-American philosopher*

What motivates you to try new approaches in your work or your community life? What resources do you read regularly to expand your knowledge and awareness of current or historical events? Here are mine. First, the Harvard Business Review and

Inc. magazine have been reading rituals for more than a decade. These monthly periodicals are full of well-researched leadership and organizational strategies for growing companies. In every issue, I find at least one article that is relevant to my practice or my clients' businesses.

Second, The Wall Street Journal is a learning source every business day. I read it before I leave for the first client meeting. Third, I end my day by reading Leadership Promises for Every Day by John C. Maxwell. My friend and colleague, Wendy Werner, calls these resources "brain candy" or information that stimulates and excites our cerebral cortex. Reading keeps you professionally relevant and vital.

For example, after reading an article in Leader to Leader, a magazine published by the Drucker Leadership Institute, I learned that CEOs wanted to read and discuss leadership challenges. I approached eight to 10 clients with this idea and the majority accepted immediately. I now host a quarterly CEO Book Club that expands my learning as well as theirs. The group's reading list includes diverse topics on leadership and organizational effectiveness. The following is a small sample of the books and articles we have read:

- "The Believer," Bo Birlingham, *Inc.* (August 1, 2008)
- *The Practice of Management,* Peter Drucker, (New York: Harper Collins Publishers, Inc., October 1954) (written in 1945)
- *Choosing Civility: The Twenty-five Rules of Considerate Conduct,* P.M. Forni, (New York: St. Martin's Press, February 2002)

• *Predictable Results in Unpredictable Times,* Stephen R. Covey, Bob Whitman, and Breck England, (Salt Lake City, Utah, Franklin Covey, September 2009)

Finally, I set a goal to read one new book each month. This ensures I have a fresh supply of options for the Book Club, as well as keeping my professional knowledge on the cutting edge. The magazines I read are my preferred sources for new book titles. If you are looking for a place to begin, *The 100 Best Business Books of All Time: What They Say, Why They Matter, and How They Can Help You* by Jack Covert and Todd Sattersten is a great resource. Developing reading rituals will add depth and dimension to your continuous learning and growth.

Catalyst 5: Teach To Learn

Stephen R. Covey, the author of numerous best-selling books and the master of the *Seven Habits of Highly Effective People*, uses a strategy called "Teach to Learn." All FranklinCovey books and workshops utilize this method to enhance knowledge retention. The method is very easy to implement. Every time you learn something, summarize the key lessons learned and share the knowledge with someone else. Research indicates that successful learning, preparation, and teaching of others leads to greater self-esteem, social connections, and self-actualization. The repetition of information also increases retention by as much as 50 percent. As a Career Equity builder, teaching expands your knowledge and presents you as a subject matter expert. Every time you teach you develop a deeper appreciation for the content and others begin to recognize you as a resource for their own learning.

Zundra is a vice president at MasterCard Worldwide. Zundra and I met several years ago when I was a panelist on career advancement for the Professional Organization of Women (P.O.W.). Her achievements are also mentioned in Chapter 8. Zundra is a master Career Equity builder. She purposefully takes knowledge and information from one context and shares it in others. For example, Zundra is a leader of MasterCard's L.E.A.D. business resource group. L.E.A.D. is dedicated to helping MasterCard employees build knowledge and relationships to advance their careers. Because of the knowledge Zundra gained from our work together at P.O.W., she recommended me as a speaker for L.E.A.D. Now, MasterCard employees are utilizing Career Equity tools (e.g., the Three-Year Letter, Career Board of Directors, etc.). Because of Zundra's learning and growth, she provided other MasterCard professionals and managers with the new tools and resources to enhance their careers. Follow Zundra's example. Learn and pass it on!

Learning And Growth Tools

Now that you understand the five catalysts Career Equity builders use to continuously learn and grow, take a moment and capture how you have been implementing these factors in your career. List one or two examples which illustrate each Learning and Growth factor in the first column of the table on Page 75.

After you complete the examples, identify the one area where you would benefit most from greater focus and attention in the next six months. Use the next tool, The Learning Action Plan on Page 75, to put your action plan in writing. Even a five percent increase in attention and intention will increase your Career Equity. Once you have established a set of learning goals for the year, create a way to track and record your learning investments. See the example on Page 76. It is also an effective record for professional organizations which require proof for accreditation and is a tangible mechanism for following-up on your intentions.

Extra Credit

1) Review *The 100 Best Business Books of All Time: What They Say, Why They Matter, and How They Can Help You,* Jack Covert and Todd Satterson, (London: Bloomsbury Publishing Inc., 2003)

3) Read *The Seven Habits of Highly Effective People*, Stephen R. Covey.

4) Create a Learning Action Plan and review it monthly.

The Learning and Growth Assessment

Learning and Growth Factor	Example(s) in the past six months	Focus Area
Catalyst 1: Embrace new opportunities		
Catalyst 2: Seek and share best practices		
Catalyst 3: Mentor or be mentored		
Catalyst 4: Cultivate a habit of reading		
Catalyst 5: Teach to learn		

Learning Action Plan Example

Event Description	Date	Credits Hours	Status
Organizational Development Conference	May 13	4	Completed
Economic Update Forum	June 30	1.5	Completed
Survey Design Workshop	September 23	3.0	Register Online
Strategy Workshop – Washington University	November 20	8.0	Registered
Total Hours (goal of 40)		*16.5*	*41.25% of goal*

5: Contributing to Community and Culture

"A man of humanity is one who, in seeking to establish himself, finds a foothold for others who, desiring attainment for himself, helps others attain."

—Confucius

"My work is challenging, I like the people I work with, and I get numerous opportunities to learn and develop new skills, but the thing that really energizes me is the time I "give back" to the community. Last year, I participated in a Habitat for Humanity build. It was rewarding to know I was creating a home for a family who might not have one."

—Senior associate at a national architecture firm

Contributing to Community and Culture is the fourth element of building Career Equity. Today, successful professionals want more from their work life than accumulating career experiences, credentials, and money. They want to know they are making a difference in the world. A recent survey of MBA students by The Aspen Institute and Net Impact found 29 percent of students surveyed have an increased interest in a career in public service. The survey report cited three themes:

• Signs point to potential increased interest in government and non-profit work among young people.

- Greater attunement to the roles of non-profits and government may help MBAs to become better social and environmental stewards.

- Non-profit management courses open students' eyes to the possibility for collaborative problem solving through cross-sector partnerships.

The interest in building Career Equity by contributing to the community is not isolated to MBAs. Nationally, the Bureau of Labor Statistics reported that from 2007 to 2012 non-profit organizations accounted for 11.4 million jobs which is 10.3 percent of all private sector employment. Additionally, 27 percent of 1.6 million graduating seniors plan to work for non-profit groups or governments, an increase of 23 percent, according to a survey of 14,225 U.S. college students conducted by the National Association of Colleges and Employers in Bethlehem, Pennsylvania. Thirty-nine percent of graduates want private sector jobs. "There's a generational shift toward increasing interest and concern about how to help make the world a better place," Amherst College President Anthony Marx said. "I hear students saying, we want to make a difference and we're not going to feel quite right about ourselves if we don't do that." (Source: Bloomberg online, June 23, 2010). What do you believe about contributing to the community? Is it a fully realized or underdeveloped aspiration?

Giving Back Builds Skills

While public service and non-profit positions fully integrate a sense of career meaning, it is not necessary to quit your job or change your career path to make a difference. Many professionals find community contribution outside their regular work day a source of fulfillment and skill building

New research conducted by Markitects in their study "Volunteering as a Pathway to Employment" provides the most compelling empirical research to date about the correlation between volunteering and employment in the United States.

For example, volunteers have a 27 percent higher likelihood of finding a job after being out of work than non-volunteers. Volunteers without a high school diploma have a 51 percent higher likelihood of finding employment. Additionally, 83 percent of respondents reported that leadership skills were honed through volunteer work and that this experience was directly transferable to their professional roles. Seventy percent of participants cited improved communication skills, and 66 percent mentioned they developed "hard skills" in fundraising and resource management. The findings indicate non-profits and community-based endeavors are an important, informal training ground for business leaders today.

Let us revisit how you scored on this rewarding career asset. See your initial assessment results on Page 17 or complete the assessment on Page 80 to explore where opportunities exist to give back and build Career Equity.

Career Asset #4 Contributing to Community and Culture Scale	Scale of 1–5
1. The organization I work for is respected in the community.	
2. I can articulate the two or three ways I would like to make a difference in the world or my community.	
3. I have written goals for my community involvement this year.	
4. I am on the Board or committee of a non-profit organization.	
5. I invite others to participate in community activities or events.	
6. I have been recognized by a community organization for my efforts.	
7. I believe community involvement enhances career growth and progression.	
8. I solicit feedback from mentors/advisors on opportunities for community involvement.	
9. My employer has a clear Purpose/Mission and Values that align with my values.	
10. I attend an "off-hours" community event at least once a month.	
Total Points for This Asset (50 possible)	

When you review your assessment, what areas stand out as strengths? Where do you have opportunities to build Career Equity while helping others? In addition, contributing to building a positive culture in your existing organization is also rewarding and gives you a broader perspective of the firms and people inside or outside your firm. The following section covers four key strategies for increasing effective community contribution.

Community Strategy #1: Know What Matters Most to You

Career Equity builders get involved and "give back." They know that doing something for the "greater good" brings multiple rewards.

As mentioned previously, "givers" gain leadership skills while building new relationships and cultivating the intrinsic satisfaction of making a difference. The issue for career-minded professionals is usually not whether to get involved but what and where to contribute. There are literally thousands of non-profit organizations who are seeking volunteer time, talent, and treasure. Which organization is an optimal fit for your skills, capabilities, and time? My guiding principle is to identify something you are passionate about.

Rewarding community contribution begins with things that matters most to you. Personally, I have a passion for the humane treatment of animals. This enthusiasm and advocacy appeared early in my life. When I was 13, I organized a petition drive to support the efforts of the *Friends of Animals*. Their mission was to expose the tuna industry for using fishing nets that inadvertently caught and suffocated dolphins. Other nets were available that could save these brilliant mammals, but they were not being used. After several years of social and political pressure by the *Friends of Animals*, the industry changed its practices and millions of dolphins are now protected. As a teenager, this community contribution taught me that getting involved, taking initiative, and organizing for action can make a valuable and sustainable change. When was the first time you recall being passionate about creating change to make something better? What lessons did you learn? What skills or competencies did you develop that are relevant to your career and life now?

More recently, my passions for helping animals led me to the Humane Society of Missouri (HSMO). A few years ago, I was reading an article in *Inc.* magazine (more evidence of the value of continuous Learning and Growth) about a woman who sold designer purses on eBay and gave the proceeds to the local humane organization. I thought it was a great idea and sent the article to the HSMO executive director. She shared my enthusiasm for the idea and asked me to spearhead a committee to "raise friends" among professional women. *Purses for Pooches and Pals* was launched. As a result more than 400 women attend this fundraiser annually. Over the past 10 years, the team has raised more than one million dollars benefitting the Dr. Doolittle Fund, which provides veterinary care for homeless, abused, and neglected animals. This event would not be possible without a strong team. In addition to the joy of achieving a significant goal for animals, I have developed new relationships with women leaders like the President of Enterprise Rent-A-Car, AT&T, and Brown Shoe Co., and others. As with other Career Equity stories, I have found when we are giving and pursuing meaningful projects, success is multiplied.

After the second year of hosting the *Purses* event, several committee members shared a desire to have a continuing role in the Humane Society mission. Out of these discussions, came the idea of forming the Women's Leadership Council (WLC) in 2007. The Council's Mission is to attract and retain women leaders who are interested in contributing to an important and sustaining project. Each year, the WLC Steering Team selects a special project such as a new rescue trailer, development of a large animal rehab facility, or "get acquainted rooms" supporting adoption services at a new Humane Society location. By hosting professional networking events the Council has grown to more than 200 members, raising $100,000 annually.

What ideas and personal passions do you have for doing good in the world that could inspire others to join you and multiply the impact of your time, talent, and treasure?

Community Strategy #2: Research The Needs In The World

Wendy Kopp, founder of Teach for America, developed the idea to eliminate educational inequity in the United States when conducting research for her senior thesis at Princeton University in 1989. Since its founding in 1990, more than 14,000 corps members have completed their commitment to Teach for America. The history of the organization is chronicled in her book *One Day, All Children: The Unlikely Triumph of Teach for America and What I Learned Along the Way.*

Community contributors like Wendy Kopp remind me of Margaret Mead's saying, "A small group of thoughtful people can change the world. Indeed, it's the only thing that ever has." If you still struggle with where to "get involved," consider the following needs awaiting your talent:

- Over seven million homeless pets in the United States need a good home.
- Most disaster fatalities happen in the aftermath of the disaster.
- America's high school graduation rate ranks 19th in the world.
- The United States is responsible for 25 percent of the carbon dioxide emissions worldwide.
- People should get at least 30 minutes of exercise at least three days a week to improve their health.
- One million people in the United States live with AIDS; one fourth are unaware of their condition.
- Over one billion people in the world live on less than one dollar a day.

Check out these websites for additional ideas:

www.volunteermatch.org

www.dosomething.org

www.getinvolved.gov

Whether child abuse, world hunger, or saving the wetlands are your passion, get involved and get involved now. The benefits to your career and the world are endless.

Community Strategy #3: Ask For Help On HOW To Get Involved

Perhaps your challenge is not what to do, but how to begin. This is where the meaningful relationships cultivated in Chapter 3 achieve additional value. I received an e-mail from the Chief Financial Officer (CFO) at a growing company who felt ready for a new challenge and opportunity to make a difference in the community. Bryan is a classic Career Equity builder. He took the initiative to reach out to me to ask for help connecting with leaders of non-profit organizations. We brainstormed his interests in education, homelessness, and places that promote family interaction (example: the Zoo or Magic House) and where his talents and expertise in finance could be of value. The next step was to identify people Bryan could network with to learn more about these organizations and their volunteer needs. Given Bryan's interest in children and education, I thought an introduction to the new president of De La Salle Middle School would be a good place to start. De La Salle's mission is to make high quality education accessible to underprivileged urban children. De La Salle is a growing organization and the Board could benefit from Bryan's financial acumen. We were able to schedule a meeting with the executive director and Board president. Bryan is now in the process of doing his "homework" and meeting with Board members to explore if this is the right place for his community contribution. Bryan knows that by taking initiative to serve others he will gain career assets through new experiences, learning, and relationships.

Community Strategy #4: Be Clear About Your Role

Like other dimensions of building Career Equity, Contributing to Community and Culture demands commitment. Once you find a place to volunteer, it is important to understand your role as a volunteer. There are numerous types of volunteer opportunities, but few places that prepare an individual for a volunteer experience. This lack of preparation often leads to an inadequate volunteer experience and disappointment. Here are four key strategies for ensuring that your investment of time and talent reaps benefits for the organization and your career:

1) **Follow through on commitments.** If you inform an agency that you will be volunteering for them, follow through with your commitment. Non-profit organizations and agencies rely heavily on the support of volunteers, and they make plans based on your promises.

2) **Show up on time.** Employees of non-profit organizations may be coordinating hundreds of different volunteers and schedules. It undermines the value of your gift if you disrupt their schedule and services.

3) **Do what is asked.** Many volunteer opportunities at non-profit organizations are not glamorous, but the role has importance. For example, the Humane Society needs volunteers to clean

out cages or make follow-up phone calls to families who recently adopted a pet. Do your homework on the volunteer assignment upfront. Remember, at the end of the day, giving is about doing what is needed instead of what is wanted, expected, or planned.

4) **Communicate a positive spirit.** Just like in your career role, people love working with volunteers with a positive attitude who are happy to serve in whatever capacity they can. In addition, many non-profits utilize long-term, enthusiastic volunteers for more complex tasks and projects. Volunteering that starts by simply stuffing envelopes often leads to larger more influential roles such as planning events, fundraisers, or being nominated to the Board of Directors.

5) **Define Your Giving Goals.** Like other dimensions of building Career Equity, you are more likely to achieve success and satisfaction if you have a plan and clear goals for your contribution. Every year when I set my business goals, I define and document my community contribution goals in specific and measurable terms. For example, I set a specific goal for personal financial contributions, investments of time, and a goal for growing the number of women who will learn about the Humane Society's mission. After each event I assess the level of our goal achievement and begin thinking about how to increase it for the following year. I know that using this discipline for me and for the committee has yielded double-digit growth of "friend and fund raising" every year for the past five years. What are your goals for giving this year?

6) **Invite Others and Expand the Envelope.** Paul Montello, managing director of Northwestern Mutual in Leawood, Kansas, does a brilliant job of blending personal and professional goals to make a profound impact on the lives of his clients, colleagues, and community. Paul is always seeking feedback on how to enhance his leadership and organization. Several years ago, we worked together on the formation of a business advisory board, similar to a Career Board of Directors, to provide Paul another source of feedback on topics such as attracting new talent to his team, client referrals, operational effectiveness, and others. Paul asked three men he respected for their professional growth, family values, high character, and willingness to help him learn and grow. All of the Board members are clients and hold C-level positions in their respective organizations. Like many business owners, Paul meets with the Board three times a year. What Paul does differently is turn this source of leadership feedback into a community giving platform. As a show of gratitude for their time and guidance, Paul donates five percent of his income to a charitable organization championed by each Board member. Organizations like Boys and Girls Club and the Good Samaritan Project have benefitted from these contributions. One of the Board members is the Executive Director of the National Center for Fathering, a passion near and dear to Paul's heart. Paul sees great synergy between the mission of the Center and his work as a business leader.

In 2014, Paul had the idea to host a Fathering Day at Lake Quivira, Kansas. The Board suggested working together to support this event and to help the National Center for Fathering expand its reach and Mission. Through his leadership and example, Paul has created a positive results multiplier. Paul gains valuable personal and professional feedback, is building meaningful relationships with values-driven leaders, and collectively, they are advancing the health and well-being of their community through generous contributions to diverse community organizations. How could you invite others to join you on a journey of growth and giving? How could you give more to gain career equity? Which of the four community strategies is a strength for you? Which one is most interesting?

As we will explore in Chapter 6, Career Equity is built through strategic action. Pick one strategy contributing to community and culture, and take one small action today.

Extra Credit:
1) Check out United Way's website at www.liveunited.org.
2) Read *The Greater Good: How Philanthropy Drives the American Economy and Can Save Capitalism,* Claire Gualdoini, (New York: Times Books, 2003).
3) Ask your Career Board of Directors about where they give and how you can make a difference.

6: Reaping the Right Recognition and Rewards

"In the arena of human life the honors and rewards fall to those who show their good qualities in action."

—*Aristotle*

R eaping the Right Recognition and Rewards is the final asset of building Career Equity. This element is last because recognition and reward are outcomes of managing, building, and cultivating a purposeful career.

A Towers Watson Global Workforce Study of more than 20,000 employees in mid-size to large companies across 22 industries reveals that competitive base pay and vacation or paid time off are among the top five career-attractiveness factors for all employees and in the top two for employees in the "Gen X and Gen Y." All too often, professionals are too passive when it comes to managing salary and benefits. Think for a moment about when you accepted your current position. Did you negotiate for a higher salary or benefits? In other words, if your employer offered $70,000 in base salary, did you ask for $75,000 or a $10,000 signing bonus or more time off? If you did, you were consciously building Career Equity. You are also in the minority. This is a Career Equity paradox. While recognition and reward are among the important and meaningful assets, many professionals do not take the initiative to understand or ask for the recognition and rewards available or that they deserve.

This lack of awareness, combined with a reluctance to ask for greater rewards, often leads to regret. When we discover peers who are more effective at research, articulating needs, and delivering results that reap greater rewards, we can be frustrated and disappointed.

Purposeful management of this asset is needed to avoid the risk of leaving significant opportunities on the table. In their widely acclaimed book, *Women Don't Ask*, Dr. Linda Babcock and Dr. Sarah Laschever illustrate the consequences for failing to manage our rewards and recognition. Their research reveals the compounded loss of a $5,000 difference in salary over a 30-year career. By failing to ask for extra compensation at the start of a career, one could lose nearly $400,000 of income during the course of a career. This does not take into account the compounding effect of money or of later promotions and progressions. While Dr. Babcock's and Dr. Laschever's research is a wake-up call to women, it is also compelling to men. While men are better at asking initially, a significant number leave money "on the table," too, and are not negotiating for the right rewards.

We have been focusing on the reward of a competitive base salary. While this asset is a forceful factor of career growth, there are other forms of recognition and reward which are most often ignored and undervalued. Career assets of tuition reimbursement, disability insurance, wellness programs and professional development funds, are just a few examples.

The critical first step of reaping the right recognition and rewards is to understand the array of rewards available and how your chosen career aligns to these options. With the accessibility of information through the Internet there is no excuse for a lack of awareness. Below are three proven resources used by Career Equity builders to conduct due diligence about career rewards:

I. Salary.com (www.salary.com)
Salary.com is all about compensation. This website offers personalized salary reports, articles, and surveys. Salary.com tools gives you a clear perspective on what employers are paying based on job title, location, experience level, and education.

II. Payscale (www.payscale.com)
Payscale provides compensation information for employers and individuals. This resource has thousands of profiles in their database. Users get free comparison reports with compensation ranges, common benefits, and job opportunities.

III. GlassDoor (www.glassdoor.com)
GlassDoor is a career community that enables job seekers to see employee opinions about a company's work environment along

with details of pay and benefits. It also has CEO approval ratings and recently launched a new section that includes reviews of job interviews.

In addition, professional associations also frequently conduct salary surveys for their membership. This is yet another way your active involvement in a professional group can help you build Career Equity. Fill out Career Asset #5 if you have not done it already.

Where do you see gaps in your reward and recognition account? With a little planning and sense of purpose you can increase your return on this career investment. How much time have you spent in the last year investigating pay, recognition, or benefits in your current or desired career? Are you fully utilizing the resources available to you? Here are five best practices to achieve greater rewards.

Five Ways To Reap Greater Rewards

1) **Conduct research or career due diligence first.** As mentioned, previously researching salaries, benefits, and other rewards, comparable to your chosen role is critical. Before you attend an interview or participate in a performance review, check your facts. Know where the high, median, and low salaries are for someone with your skills, experience, and education. When you are considering a career change, make sure to ask the people in your newly chosen field questions about compensation. Ask them to help you set realistic

Career Asset #5 Reaping the Right Rewards and Recognition	Scale of 1–5
1. In the past month, I received recognition or praise for my work.	
2. I know the market value of pay and benefits for my position and experience.	
3. I use at least 70 percent or more of my annual vacation time each year.	
4. I participate in a 401K program or other retirement savings plan.	
5. I am fully informed about my health care benefits: medical, dental, life insurance, and long-term disability.	
6. I am satisfied with my level of base pay compensation.	
7. I have a high degree of flexibility in choosing when I take time off for vacation, etc.	
8. My organization makes contributions to charities or organizations I believe in.	
9. The people I work with want me to succeed and advance.	
10. In the past month, I have given recognition or praise to a co-worker.	
Total Points for This Asset (50 possible)	

expectations for differences in compensation due to roles and responsibilities, company size, and industry. Do not assume that salary and/or benefits are not negotiable. Remember that benefits can equal up to 25 percent of any employment package. Negotiating salary prior to having a detailed understanding of a company's benefit package may prove costly.

Research reveals that the majority of employers expect you to negotiate. Many consider it a test of assertiveness and initiative.

2) Consider the whole package. Remember to add benefits such as educational reimbursements, vacation time, and travel allowances in your negotiations. These are elements of your entire reward package and are often overlooked. Do not get hung up on base salary. Benefits that make your life easier, increase skill sets, or save you time necessary to accelerate your Career Equity and may also be easy for your employer to implement. Doing your rewards homework on the entire employment package also speaks volumes about you. It says you manage from facts; you are purposeful about your career, and have the courage to seek a win-win. If you have worked in one firm for several years, now may be a good time to review your company benefit options. Schedule a time to speak with a Human Resources professional to get an update. In today's dynamic business environment, rewards change quickly. Being informed is a key step to accumulating greater career wealth.

3) **Monitor the pulse of your industry.** Make sure that your skills, experience, and education are properly aligned with your discipline. This is further evidence for the importance of Career Equity Asset #3 – Relentlessly Pursuing Learning and Growth. Continually reading about trends in your industry keeps you on the leading edge and prepares you for new opportunities. For example, one of my general contracting clients works with WalMart. By staying on top of industry trends, they recognized the opportunity to expand services to other national retailers (e.g., Target, Kohl's, etc.). The reward: The client's team now has a new division focused on national retailing and the individual who identified the opportunity has great Career Equity – he is now the Senior Vice President leading the group.

4) **Point out your value and seek a win-win.** When negotiating rewards and recognition, discuss how you can and will contribute to the organization's desired results, and not simply what you want. Provide concrete examples of how your skills and contributions support the company's goals. This increases the probability of achieving mutual value. For example, one professional was able to demonstrate how his networking in a professional organization led to recruitment of three new sales reps. Another professional made the correlation between a presentation given and how it resulted in bringing a new client to the firm. In both cases, the initia-

tive and activity achieved a result. One my clients is fond of borrowing Peter Drucker's quote, "Leadership is defined by results." While employers value effort, they pay for results. Keep track of results you are achieving so you can make a compelling case for win-win rewards. Never make a one-sided reward request focused exclusively on your needs. Leaders do not want to hear that you are behind on your mortgage or have kids going to college. Leave personal needs out of negotiations.

5) **Give often.** Another positive Career Equity paradox is that giving leads to more rewards. Teach a class, mentor someone, or give your knowledge away. When I read a compelling article, I send it to clients and colleagues I think will benefit from the information. I also publish a quarterly e-newsletter to provide colleagues and clients with best practices, new books, tools, or resources that advance their goals. In addition to the intrinsic satisfaction of helping others, this sharing has resulted in new members to my CEO Book Club, new clients, and opportunities to speak at national organization meetings. As Brian Tracy, author and guru on human potential says: "Develop an attitude of gratitude, and give thanks for everything that happens to you, knowing that every step forward is a step toward achieving something bigger and better than your current situation." Here are a few examples of how to give that make your career experience richer and more rewarding:

- Volunteer to be a coach or be the "go-to person" for a new member of the firm or project team.
- Offer to take notes at a team meeting or learning conference and publish the summary for other team members.
- Organize a community event such as a "fundraiser" for the United Way or another cause of interest.
- Send a note of appreciation to firm leaders for sponsoring a fun event.

What are you giving away? All of these career rewards and recognition are a function of giving ideas and knowledge to others. Take a few minutes and brainstorm giving ideas that are relevant and energizing to you or your organization. Then pick one and put it into action.

Note: *You would be amazed how few professionals acknowledge these efforts and how much they are valued by the leaders who rarely receive positive upward feedback.*

Investing In Your Future Now – Contributing To 401K

When I started my career at McDonnell Douglas Corporation, the company matched every dollar I saved in the 401K program with stock. In other words, if I saved one dollar, they would deposit a dollar of stock in my retirement account. As a Human Resources professional, I had access to reports of employee participation in this program. Less than 30 percent of all employees who had the option to participate did so.

When I left the organization seven years later, McDonnell Douglas was sold to The Boeing Company and the stock had split three times during my tenure. In other words, I left with three times the stock I had contributed. What was even more amazing is that when I went to Arthur Andersen, I found the same dynamic in play. I assumed that smart financially savvy CPAs would understand the value of compounded savings. Again, only 34 percent of employees participated in the firm's 401K program. This is not isolated to big firms or companies. In the United States, the individual savings rate is only about four percent; this is up from one percent in the last five years. Career Equity builders are not satisfied with these results. They want to fully utilize every tool at their disposal to increase tangible and intangible rewards.

Investigate the savings options available to you today. Many organizations have an intranet with a description of employee benefits. Take the initiative to meet with your firm's Human Resources professionals. Either way, find out what savings options are available to you and begin or increase your contribution. The smallest amount invested today yields great Career Equity in the future. Also, when you leave or change jobs remember to "roll-over" these investments. Seek the guidance of a financial services advisor to explore how the equity you have built can be accumulated and combined with equity you will accumulate in your new role or company.

The Reward Of Paid Time Off – Are You Taking It?

Let us examine another reward that is often underappreciated: vacation or paid time off. According to a New York Times' "Vacation Deprivation" survey, many Americans do not use all of their paid time away from work. The survey reveals that on average, workers will likely lose up to three days of vacation time annually.

Additionally, according to the findings of a survey by travel site Expedia.com of 1,301 workers, employers get about 415 million vacation days returned to them. Even those that do use their vacation time say that they are checking their e-mail or office voice mail while they are off. Nearly one-third (32 percent) say they work while on vacation. The average vacation allotment for workers was 12.4 days a year. Losing two to three days a year over a 20-year career is nearly two months of pay. If someone offered you two months of free pay would you take it? More importantly, unplugging from work on a regular basis has been shown to increase energy, creativity, and outlook about work.

Health Care Bane Or Benefit?

In an affluent culture like the United States, employer-paid health care has become a career entitlement. The high cost of health care combined with broad changes in health care reform will undoubtedly change the valence or level of importance of this Career Equity factor in years to come.

According to the 2014, Employer Health Benefits Survey released by the Kaiser Family Foundation, health care premiums increased by more than six percent or triple the rate of wage growth. In 2014, the average annual premiums for employer-sponsored health insurance were $6,025 for single coverage and $16,834 for family coverage. Over the past 10 years, average premiums for family coverage have increased 69 percent. "Working people don't feel like they are getting any relief because their premiums have been rising faster than their paychecks," says Foundation President Drew Altman. Being informed and engaged with your health care benefits enhances Career Equity. How much does your employer plan save you? Do you fully understand COBRA benefits if your career exit is unplanned (e.g., layoff)? Take the time to review health care options and the cost of premiums to you and your employer.

The Right Recognition

Is receiving recognition important to you? A Harris poll asked, "What two or three things do you want most in a job?" "Recognition for a job well done" was in the top three. Additionally, in a recent *Workforce* article, Bob Nelson, a nationally known recognition guru, said "More than anything else, employees want to be valued for a job well done by those they hold in high esteem."

While we highly value recognition, most professionals are not proactive in getting it. Rather, it can seem arbitrary and outside of our control. To increase the thoughtful recognition you receive, you must model the behavior you want. Mahatma Gandhi's wisdom is relevant here: "Be the change you want to see in the world." When was the last time you recognized a peer or colleague for a job well done? How do you feel when you express appreciation in a sincere and thoughtful way? Giving meaningful recognition has an immediate intrinsic benefit to you and the receiver. As with many dimensions of Career Equity, it results in mutual growth. Here are a few recognition practices that deliver the right rewards:

1) **Develop a weekly discipline of writing one handwritten note of appreciation to someone.** In our high-tech world, high-touch habits such as note writing have diminished. How many times have you kept a handwritten note or card someone sent you? In my experience, they are superior to e-mail. Cultivating this discipline improves positive proactive communication and builds meaningful relationships.

2) **Research award and recognition traditions in your company or community and go for one.** Awards and incentive programs are designed to highlight behaviors that matter most to company results. Company leaders have a defined win-win in these programs. For example, the Barry Wehmiller organization awards the use of a company Chevrolet SSR for a week to an employee who is nominated by peers for exceptional performance. Winning these awards can be fun, engage peers, and depending on their significance, can

differentiate you from others. For example, in the financial security industry, the Million Dollar Round Table (MDRT) is earned by fewer than 10 percent of all financial services professionals. Once achieved, it is recognition with meaning to the individual, their clients, and their income.

Many professionals ask me how to gain recognition awarded by local business journals (e.g., Most Influential Business Women, or Top 30 Under 30, or Fastest Growing Firm award, etc.). First, know the criteria for the award and determine its relevance to your skills, talents, and aspirations. Second, apply or ask someone to nominate you and do so in a timely manner. You would be amazed at the number of people who are not eligible because they do not meet the deadline. Provide nominators with all the background information needed to help them make a positive impression on your behalf. Third, follow-up to ensure all relevant information is received. Send notes of congratulations to those who receive the award, even if you do not. Remember to recognize the people who contributed to your success. Few, if any of us, achieve great results alone. The purpose of this chapter is to optimize the recognition and rewards most compelling to you. Career Equity builders know what motivates them. They are informed about the pay, benefits, and perquisites (tangible or intangible) and achieve them with intention and purpose.

Recently, I received an email from a professional who is very purposeful about enhancing her tangible recognition and rewards. She is an employee development director, or internal coach, to financial advisors. She works hard to develop and provide them with systems, tools, and challenging feedback to help them achieve their business goals. She had the feeling that her work was not realizing rewards comparable to other leaders in her role. We discussed a plan for her to research peer compensation, the rewards she wanted, and to quantify the impact her work has on business results. In other words, she needed to know, in specific terms, how helping financial advisors achieve a greater percentage of their goals benefited the managing director's revenue. After our interaction, she completed a thorough review of peer rewards and the organization's results. She sent me an analysis of these factors and solicited my feedback to give her another perspective. This is a great example of how to use a mentor or accountability advisor in the process. After we discussed a few changes, we did a role play of how she would present her findings and recommendations to the managing director. The next step was to schedule a meeting with the managing director, present her thoughts and findings, and solicit his feedback.

Remember achieving the right recognition and rewards is about finding the win-win. She needed to articulate her needs in a way that demonstrated how the organization benefits when she gets the rewards she wants. Her story illustrates what Career Equity building is all about. She identified gaps in her career satisfaction, researched the facts, organized a solution, and solicited feedback from mentors or experienced leaders to improve her strategy. Her approach will yield an increase in her compensation. Most importantly, it increases the intangible asset of empowering herself to articulate her needs and see an improved result.

Where can you gain greater reward and recognition for your career contributions? Would taking some well-earned time off, investing in your firm's sponsored 401K, or negotiating a pay increase take your career satisfaction to the next level? Pick one area that would create a great return on your investment, and like the Nike slogan says, "Just Do It."

Extra Credit:

1) Read *Women Don't Ask: Negotiation and the Gender Divide,* Linda Babcock and Sarah Laschever (Princeton, NJ: Princeton University Press, 2003).

2) Check out *101 Ways to Stand Out at Work: How to Get the Recognition and Rewards You Deserve,* Arthur D. Rosenberg (Avon, MA: Adams Media and F+W Media Company, 2009).

3) Nominate a colleague for a special recognition in your firm or community.

7: Putting Action and Accountability Behind Aspirations

"The Common Denominator of Success – the secret of success of every person who has ever been successful – lies in the fact that they formed the habit of doing things that failures don't like to do."

—Albert E.N. Gray

Great rewards await those who define goals and act purposefully to achieve them. Dr. Gail Matthews, a professor in Dominican's Department of Psychology in the School of Arts, Humanities and Social Sciences, recruited 267 participants from a wide variety of businesses, organizations, and networking groups throughout the United States and overseas for a study on how goal achievement in the workplace is influenced by writing goals, committing to goal-directed actions, and accountability for those actions. Participants ranged in ages from 23 to 72 and represented a wide spectrum of backgrounds. Matthews found that more than 70 percent of the participants who sent weekly updates to a friend reported successful goal achievement (completely accomplished their goal or were more than half way there), compared to 35 percent of those who kept their goals to themselves, without writing them down. If you are investing the time and resources to read this book you are clearly in the 70 percent.

On the surface it is deceptively simple. However, like most noteworthy efforts, it demands something extra. The important thing to know is that this capacity is learned and can be taught to others.

As Dr. Matthew's research reveals, those who achieve abundance foster a habit of thinking about their aspirations and gain support from others. They relentlessly keep score of their progress. What does your goal review discipline reveal today? How often do you think about these goals? What accountability do you have in place to act on them – every day? To convert your career aspirations into reality, you need to create and sustain four goal-achievement habits:

Habit #1 – Get Organized. Create a place where all of your career goals, ideas, and action plans are kept. If it sounds fundamental, it is. I see business leaders every day that have piles of forms, goals, and Post-it notes with ideas, but lack the organization to move goals forward quickly.

Organize a written document which includes your "vital" career goals and plans for the next year. Be as creative and imaginative as you want. Some professionals use pictures and images with written goals to help them "see" their ultimate success. The critical element of this habit is to ensure the goals are measurable and achievable and kept in a location where you will review the goals frequently. I have a one-page description of my annual goals in a notebook I carry with me daily.

I mention "vital" goals. Fewer than seven is ideal. It is difficult to work on more than seven goals concurrently and achieve significance. Less in goal setting is truly more. The following is an example of a well-defined goal: After assessing his Career Equity in Asset 3, relentless Learning and Growth, Bob set a goal to achieve a Chartered Financial Analyst (CFA) accreditation by December 2017. The goal is specific, measurable, achievable, and time-oriented; all elements of an effective career goal. Most importantly, it aligns with Bob's assessment and aspiration to build more Career Equity in Learning and Growth.

Habit #2 – Convert Long-Term Goals to Short-Term Action Steps. While we love thinking of long-term dreams or aspirations, it is action that turns goals into reality. The following commonly held professional achievement illustrates the point. Graduating from college is a long-term career aspiration that requires a minimum of four and up to 10 years (if you pursue a PhD or medical degree) to achieve. To earn a "walk across the stage" and receive a college diploma, demands hundreds, if not thousands, of action steps.

If we attended to all those steps when we began, we would be overwhelmed and never complete our goal. This may be why, according to the 2014 United States Census, that only 31 percent of adults succeed in achieving a Bachelor's degree and fewer than 11 percent graduate with a Masters or PhD. Those who succeed learn how to focus their time and attention on actions required in the present. For example, each semester you want to attend college, you must register for courses. If you were intent and organized in this process, you typically got the courses you wanted at the time of day and with your preferred professor. If you procrastinated and did not follow a purposeful action plan, it is likely your class schedule was less than ideal. This result demonstrates the differential impact of actions taken on purpose or those taken by accident. With simple planning and action, we can optimize our life and performance. Let us apply this insight to building equity in your career portfolio today.

Let us say you want to enhance a relationship with a leader or mentor in your organization and build more equity by cultivating meaningful relationships. Your action plan might look like the table on Page 111.

How long do you think it took to define this action plan? Answer: About 10 to 15 minutes to organize. I share this because often the first response to organizing is "I don't have time for that." We spend more energy fighting against a new habit or discipline than simply doing it.

Take 10 minutes to organize your actions and see how you feel when the plan is outlined.

The action plan on Page 111 contains specific, deadline driven, realistic steps that can be achieved in the time frame outlined. A great deal is written on how to create action plans. You can surf the web for various strategies. Discover the approach that works best for you. The most essential step is to write them down and put them in a place where you can find them and review them easily.

Goal, Aspiration, or Desired Result	Actions	By When	Status
Build a stronger relationship with …	1. Schedule an in-person meeting	No later than Sept. 30th	
	2. Prepare several questions or issues I want feedback on during our meeting	September 15th	
	3. Make reservations for lunch at restaurant	September 18th	
	4. Send follow-up note or thank you for their time	Day after lunch	
	5. Send a status note on issues we discussed and how I have acted on their feedback	30 days after lunch	

Habit #3 – Develop a Systematic Review of Goals and Results. The third and most important habit to form is the systematic review of goals and results. This is what separates good goal achievers from great goal achievers. Human behavior often works against consistent, relentless effort. We love the next new thing, idea, and so on. Systematically reviewing an action plan demands self-discipline as well as the ability to confront disappointment and delay gratification. While writing a well-defined action plan increases the probability of achieving our goals, the regular and consistent review keeps us focused, honest, and bothered when we are not progressing. The tension that occurs when we realize actions not taken is the fuel or motivation to get us back on track. Those who build high Career Equity and accomplish significant goals have the courage to confront the gap between what they said they would do (aspiration) and what they are doing (reality).

Here Is An Ideal Review Schedule And Checklist:

Monthly – Schedule about 30 minutes each month to review all of your annual goals and Vision or Three-Year Letter. Check in on how your aspirations are progressing and identify the things that need action in the next 30 days.

Weekly – Create another 30-minute investment of time to align the week ahead to monthly actions. Like a chiropractor making small adjustments, you will achieve the biggest positive changes in the long-term for honoring this discipline. For example, if one of your monthly goals is to attend a professional credential workshop, decide what can be done this week to advance that goal. Can I submit the registration form this week or review the pre-work materials? When I do my weekly planning on Sunday evenings, I pull out my schedule for the week ahead along with my goals and ask myself the following questions:

When this week is over, what will I feel great about achieving? What would make me feel that I have used my time effectively and advanced some part of my longer-term aspirations? I have a one-page form where I record my "Desired Results" for the week and check several times a week to track my progress and reconcile accomplished goals with those not met.

Here are a few examples of what you would see on my weekly Desired Results list:

- Write a one-page case study on goal achievement for clients and post on website.
- Exercise aerobically 3x and practice yoga on Saturday.
- Document a client-strategic plan and send to the leadership team.

Daily – Spend five to 10 minutes at the beginning of each day creating a "To Do" list. The art and science of this action and accountability tool is to ensure the other two review habits are implemented. Many people generate a "To Do" list in isolation. Without a context for longer-term aspirations, a "To Do" list can be an energy vampire. The endless lists of tasks and effort can be daunting. But when we put our goals in the context of our

Vision, we are motivated and energized about the rewards of the tasks. They have a context and a purpose. Those who systematically review their goals monthly, weekly, and daily have high Career Equity, are extremely satisfied, and often arrive at aspirations ahead of schedule. If all of these tools leave you feeling overwhelmed, pick one habit that is most relevant and try it for the next 30 days.

Habit #4 – Invoke Accountability Advisors. The fourth and final habit is to cultivate the practice of asking for accountability from those who want you to succeed. This habit is often more difficult than it sounds for independent goal-oriented professionals. Yet the rewards are exponential. Who in your life holds you accountable for realizing your goals and being the best version of yourself? Who has the courage to give you feedback about what you need to do differently? The following story is a best practice, from three professionals who seized the opportunity to bring their Three-Year Letter to life by making a commitment to themselves and each other. Zundra Bryant, Vice President, MasterCard; Gail Taylor, Brand Manager, Energizer Holdings, Inc.; and Sarajeni Hammond, Talent Management Lead, Monsanto, are very intentional about their career goals and support each other in achieving them. After participating in a Career Equity learning session that is part of the St. Louis Business Diversity Initiative Fellows Program, this purposeful trio committed to meet once a month for three years to review their goals and aspirations. Yes, I said once each month for three years!

They believed that holding each other accountable would increase the probability of achieving their goals. They were right. Their success was so compelling the *St. Louis Business Journal* wrote an article highlighting their achievements. (See September 12, 2014, issue).

"We formed our Building Career Equity Accountability group to formalize a support system that would enable us to achieve the goals outlined in our Three-Year Letters. Our Accountability Group serves as a source of motivation and additional responsibility to stay focused on our long-term goals in the midst of managing our daily lives. We encourage one another to take risks, challenge each other's mindsets and paradigms, and celebrate our successes. Our partnership is a source of strength and a solid foundation for pursuing our career equity!" said Zundra Bryant.

When I asked Zundra what she valued most about the Accountability Group she said, "The power of the written word! Shortly after we finished writing our Three-Year Letters, each of us achieved a major milestone. It was absolutely amazing. My confidence level has increased exponentially and I'm a stronger professional at work. I know my accountability partners are there for me, no matter what. It's liberating. Going into our last year, I'm contemplating how to dream bigger and figure out how to stretch myself further."

Nathaniel Branden, internationally known author of the *Six Pillars of Self-Esteem* writes, "No one is coming to save you." Career Equity builders, like Zundra, Gail, and Sarajeni, take the initiative to ask for support and accountability. The "ask" is a reflection of strength and clarity for personal and professional growth. This is not a strategy to get others to do your work for you. It is your work and career goals supported by those who want you to succeed. I put this habit last because it is most effective when the first three habits are in place. When you are organized, have specific action plans, and systematically review your goals, your request to others can be energizing for them and for you. You will be specific about what you want and what you need to succeed. Zundra, Gail, and Sarajeni used their monthly meetings as a way to get new ideas about how to build their skills, and most importantly, self-efficacy.

Because Zundra, Gail, and Sarajeni had a vision of what they wanted to achieve, organized their actions, and took the initiative to seek feedback, they achieved many of their stated goals.

Who would benefit from knowing about your goals and how would that knowledge and support help you? When will you take the initiative to ask for the added accountability to make your career goals a reality?

I want to close this chapter on action and accountability with an excerpt from *The Common Denominator of Success* written by Albert E. N. Gray. It was part of his address in 1940 to the National Life Underwriter's Association at their annual convention in Philadelphia.

This speech is avidly read by the best professionals in the financial-security business today. Gray's insights about what differentiates goal achievers are relevant to any professional, in any organization, and at any time:

> "Any resolution or decision you make is simply a promise to you. It isn't worth a tinker's dam unless you have formed the habit of making it and keeping it. And you won't form the habit of making it and keeping it unless right at the start you link it with a definite purpose that can be accomplished by keeping it. In other words, any resolution or decision you make today has to be made again tomorrow, and the next day, and the next, and the next, and so on. And it not only has to be made each day, but it has to be kept each day, for if you miss one day in the making or keeping of it, you've got to go back and begin all over again. But if you continue the process of making it each morning and keeping it each day, you will finally wake up some morning a different person in a different world, and you will wonder what has happened to you and the world you used to live in."

Extra Credit

1) Read *Getting Things Done,* David Allen, (New York: Penguin Group, 2001).
2) Read *The New Common Denominator of Success,* Albert E. N. Gray, (Albany, Oregon: May 2008).
3) Organize a time to do weekly planning for 30 minutes.

8: Cultivating a Career Equity Culture

"Someone's sitting in the shade today because someone planted a tree a long time ago."

—*Warren Buffett*

Dear Firm Leader Or Manager,

If you are reading this, I know you have a desire to build an organization that provides professionals with a unique and meaningful career experience. You understand the connection between professional growth/retention and organizational performance. Most importantly, you believe that creating an organizational culture demands a clear purpose and relentless implementation of proven practices.

This chapter is written exclusively for leaders like you who desire, know, and believe that mutually beneficial relationships with professionals are the catalyst to growth and firm effectiveness. While professionals can and will benefit from mastering the Career Equity model individually, exponential growth comes from implementing these practices throughout your organization. This chapter provides you with proven practices and disciplines needed to cultivate a Career Equity Culture; a culture that attracts, and most importantly, retains the best talent for your organization and requires different ways of thinking and communicating. Many of your peers do not know about these practices. At least their behavior does not reflect that they do.

However, an enlightened subset of the nation's best professional firms and companies have implemented the Career Equity philosophy systematically and are reaping the rewards. They achieve a greater market share of the best recruits and their average tenure of the best professionals exceeds competitors by more than two years. They have also recognized a measurable increase in profitability. You are also likely to find them on "The Best Places to Work" lists. Would you like your firm to realize greater results in these areas?

If you are like most leaders, you have heard and read the statistics. You know that the average tenure of professional talent within any one organization is approximately 2.5 years and that profitability drops when the recruiting, training, and development investments you have made walk out the door for greener pastures. A global workforce study, conducted by Towers Watson (2010), found that more than 89 percent of employees believe career management is their responsibility, but they also report that only about 30 percent get adequate support from managers to realize their aspirations. More alarming is that nearly 60 percent consult their peers when making a decision to stay or go. Peers are not the only people you want guiding the career choices of top performers.

Let us take a look at the way you collaborate with professionals. What percentage of the people in your organization consider you or one of your leaders a trusted career advisor? How many would be the first to tell you if they received an offer from one of your competitors? What mechanisms are in place to have purposeful conversations about each professional's career vision?

The Road Map For Creating Such A Place Is Here

The first step to cultivating a Career Equity culture requires knowing what matters most to each professional. This means having a planned and intentional career discussion with every person in your company or firm. This is not an annual performance review. Understanding the career goals and aspirations of the people important to your enterprise demands more than a meeting once a year. This conversation begins in the recruiting process and should persist throughout a professional's work in your firm. On average, leaders who are reaping the rewards of a Career Equity culture meet with professionals four times a year to check in on career goals, achievement, and satisfaction. However, they do not get hung up on the frequency of meetings. They know that the most important thing is to understand, in explicit terms, what energizes each professional. Further, they are relentless about ensuring professionals have the right relationships to support their career achievement.

The examples on the next page are provided for both experienced and campus recruiting. Several are relevant for career conversations after professionals are onboard too.

Experienced Recruiting:

- Tell me about your career experience to this point. What are the two to three things that you enjoy most about your work? What two to three things that are challenging for you at this stage of your career?

- Our business is all about client service. Our people are professionals that value serving and pleasing clients. If I were to contact a few of your clients, what would they say are your two or three strengths? In other words, why do they like to work with you?

- What would your managers or partners say are your two or three areas for growth and development?

- What achievement in your career are you most proud of and why?

- Tell me about a time you had to serve leaders who had competing needs or demands. How did you resolve the conflict of time/resources?

Campus Recruiting:

- Tell me about a time when you had to take the lead in a team or project. What challenges did you confront in this new role? How did you overcome them?

- What were your favorite courses in college and why?

- Which courses were more challenging or least energizing for you?

- Tell me about experiences where you were in a leadership role. What did you learn from giving direction to others?

- Did you work during college? What skills did you gain from this experience? How do you think those experiences could relate to the opportunity you are pursuing with our firm?

ZeroDay Technology Solutions (ZDTS) provides a great example of how firm leaders can integrate Career Equity into their selection process and reap value for the firm, their people and clients. Everyone knows technology professionals are in great demand and recruiting efforts must be compelling to entice experienced candidates to consider new and growing organizations over established brands. While the ZDTS team is relatively new, they are dedicated to ensuring a long-term career fit with the people they hire. Director of MiCiV Solutions, Bill Orr, conducts an in-depth interview with each candidate highlighting specific Career Equity dimensions (e.g., engaging work, relationships, learning and community engagement, the right recognition and rewards) and ZeroDay team members share their ZDTS Career Equity experiences.

Bill is passionate about this process because of the results he and the team are achieving. "It is amazing how impressive the concept is to candidates and how it takes the discussion to a more thoughtful and meaningful level. Several candidates have told us that the focus on their Career Equity differentiated ZDTS from other opportunities they were considering," Bill said. More importantly, ZDTS leadership backs up the selection process with a commitment to support and advance the career growth of professionals after being hired. Leadership offers regular one-on-one Career Equity sessions with each team member, both formal and informal. Employees are asked to score themselves and the organization according to the matrices in the Career Equity book. Each team member is required to write a Three-Year Letter and is given the option to share it or keep it private. Most choose to share, which has prompted meaningful, and at times, emotional conversations between team members and leaders. In a high growth environment with many priorities for leaders and professionals to focus on, why does the ZDTS team make this investment? Bill shared, "We have found it to be an empowering tool that allows us to better understand the motivators and point of view of our people. The benefit to the business is that employee retention becomes about relationships, with a focus on long-term career paths, instead of simple wages and benefits. This is a critical advantage in the IT industry which is known for aggressive recruiting practices and significant salary increases."

What mechanisms do you use to understand the aspirations of potential team members? How do you carry this understanding through the entire career experience in your firm? Consider the ZDTS solution of developing a meaningful understanding of each professional's aspirations from recruitment to retirement.

Another example of how Career Equity can shape an organization's culture early in the people development cycle is to utilize the tools and questions in the college marketing or intern selection process. At Northwestern Mutual, leaders know that college interns who commit to a full-time career have better long-term retention and productivity than any other source of hiring. For this reason, the company has a strategy of ensuring that more than 50 percent of new recruits will come from college hiring by the year 2020. There are more than 230 District Offices within Northwestern Mutual working to implement this goal.

Finding a differentiating strategy is critical to achieving a firm's market share of the best interns from the most competitive colleges and universities. Just ask Paul Montello, Managing Director of the Northwestern office in Leawood, Kansas. Paul and his College Marketing leader are passionate about helping interns realize their career aspirations by providing them with trusted career advisors early in their professional careers. Paul decided the Building Career Equity model was a perfect framework for designing a unique college intern experience. Using the five assets of Career Equity: (1) Engaging Work, (2) Meaningful Relationships, (3) Learning and Growth, (4) Community and Culture, and (5) The Right Recognition and Rewards, they developed a tangible and customized experience for each intern to gather career assets.

For example, each intern is assigned a "Joint-Work" partner or an experienced advisor who guides them in learning the business and facilitating client relationships. Additionally, interns are encouraged to participate in firm-sponsored community events like Alex's Lemonade Stand (a non-profit organization whose mission is to raise resources to fight childhood cancer causes and fund research into new treatments and cures).

The Director of College Marketing meets with interns to track their individual Career Equity progress throughout the summer experience. Is college recruiting or marketing a key driver of your firm's growth? What makes your program unique? How would interns say that you are helping them build trusted relationships to enhance their career growth? As in Chapter 1, where each professional is invited to assess his or her current level of career effectiveness, the best place for leaders to begin building a Career Equity culture is to assess how the organization is providing professionals with the resources to cultivate and grow their careers. The Career Equity Culture Assessment (See pages 128-132) will help you and your leaders identify firm strengths and places for optimizing career development strategies. The actual numbers are less important than the awareness and alignment that is derived from having a purposeful conversation about the firm's culture.

Career Equity Culture Assessment: Using a scale where 10 = very true of our firm's practices today, 5 = somewhat true of our firm today, and 1 = not at all true of our organization's career practices today, read each of the statements and place the appropriate rating in the box to the right of the statement. Creating a Career Equity Culture is achieved over time and with systematic attention to the growth and development of each professional. The following guidelines will help you evaluate your organization's current level of effectiveness.

Evaluation Guidelines

- Scores between 45 and 50 in a category indicate exceptional investment and commitment to professional career growth. The firm has a competitive advantage in this area.

- Scores that fall between 35 and 44 in a category indicate intentional effort and energy are in place to accelerate professional career success. The firm enjoys several best practices in this area.

- Scores that fall between 25 and 34 in a category indicate that a moderate level of attention is given to helping professionals advance career growth. The firm would benefit from a higher level of leadership focus and commitment to career development strategies.

- Any category total of 24 or less indicates a need for attention and an actionable plan.

While having exceptional scores in every area is desirable, it is not typical.

Career Asset #1 Providing Engaging Work	Scale of 1 – 10
1. We know the career vision of every professional in our firm, and they are written for future reference.	
2. Each professional has a measurable set of goals for things that are most important to accomplish, and this is reviewed on a regular basis with a firm leader or manager.	
3. Each professional's work reflects a high degree of autonomy and independence.	
4. We measure the career satisfaction of every professional in a systematic way.	
5. Our recruitment practices intentionally measure the fit between candidate career aspirations and the needs of our organization.	
Total Points for This Asset (50 possible)	

*This component measures the extent to which the firm is Providing **Engaging Work** for professionals. After completing an individual assessment, compare your results with other partners, associates, and/or Human Resource leaders. What patterns and trends emerge from an integrated assessment of the firm's current state? Note observations and questions that emerged as you completed the assessment:*

_____

_____

_____

_____

Career Asset #2 Cultivating Meaningful Relationships	Scale of 1 – 10
1. We know the names of each professional's mentors or career advisors in our company or firm.	
2. We coach professionals to build an effective network of colleagues, inside and outside the firm.	
3. We have a system or practice for soliciting feedback from each professional about how to improve mentor relationships in our firm.	
4. Our mentors or career advisors meet with professionals, at least quarterly, on an individual basis.	
5. Mentors and career advisors receive specific training and skill development.	
Total Points for This Asset (50 possible)	

*This component measures the extent to which the firm provides opportunities for **Cultivating Meaningful Relationships.** After completing an individual assessment, compare your results with other partners, associates, and/or Human Resource leaders. What patterns and trends emerge from an integrated assessment of the firm's current state? Note observations and questions that emerged as you completed the assessment:*

Career Asset #3 Relentlessly Pursuing Learning and Growth	Scale of 1 – 10
1. Each professional has a formal learning, growth, and development plan with specific measurable goals.	
2. Professionals are encouraged to teach or facilitate training/learning programs at least once a year.	
3. Our performance management system requires each professional to complete a self-evaluation.	
4. There is an intentional link between career goals and work assignments/projects.	
5. Department or company training budgets are allocated to ensure the best professionals are receiving the right learning and growth and are reviewed for implementation regularly.	
Total Points for This Asset (50 possible)	

*This component measures the extent to which the firm provides opportunities for **Relentlessly Pursuing Learning and Growth.** After completing an individual assessment, compare your results with other partners, associates, and/or Human Resource leaders. What patterns and trends emerge from an integrated assessment of the firm's current state? Note observations and questions that emerged as you completed the assessment:*

Career Asset #4 Contributing to Community and Culture	Scale of 1 – 10
1. Our organization promotes the success of civic and non-profit organizations (events, donations, etc.).	
2. We provide time away from work for our professionals to participate in "giving back" (e.g., Habit for Humanity building project).	
3. We have written "giving goals" for the company and encourage professionals to set individual goals.	
4. Our organization has a positive reputation in the community for giving and contributing.	
5. Our leaders serve on boards or committees of non-profit organizations in our community.	
Total Points for This Asset (50 possible)	

*This component measures the extent to which the firm provides opportunities for **Contributing to Community and Culture**. After completing an individual assessment, compare your results with other partners, associates, and/or Human Resource leaders. What patterns and trends emerge from an integrated assessment of the firm's current state? Note observations and questions that emerged as you completed the assessment:*

Career Asset #5 The Right Recognition and Rewards	Scale of 1 – 10
1. We teach leaders and mentors how to make recognition and praise personal and meaningful.	
2. We provide our professionals with tools to evaluate the market value of pay and benefits compared to competitors.	
3. Professionals have a high degree of autonomy in scheduling vacations and are encouraged by firm leaders to use it.	
4. We offer a 401K program and at least 80 percent of our firm members participate.	
5. We provide comprehensive health care coverage; dental, life insurance, and long-term disability insurance.	
Total Points for This Asset (50 possible)	

This component measures the extent to which the firm provides **The Right Recognition and Rewards.** *After completing an individual assessment, compare your results with other partners, associates, and/or Human Resource leaders. What patterns and trends emerge from an integrated assessment of the firm's current state? Note observations and questions that emerged as you completed the assessment:*

_____

_____

_____

_____

Organizations purposeful about creating a Career Equity culture over the long-term will focus on the vital few areas where improvement is needed and work to do so! After reviewing your scores in each area, what stands out to you about the current state of your Career Equity culture? Which of the assets yielded the highest number of points? Which asset has the fewest number of points? Cultivating a culture of career growth demands purposeful processes and behaviors. Cynicism is alive and well in organizations today because many leaders say that people and career growth are "their most important asset" and then behave in ways that are incongruent with this intention. Many espouse "career concern," but as the research indicates, few are masters at putting it into practice.

What Does A Career Equity Culture Look Like?

How do leaders begin to create an organization that gives professionals unique learning, relationships, and engagement? How can we implement an approach that makes a lasting impact on our people and firm? How can we know that the career management investments we make are yielding our desired results? If you are asking these questions, you are on the right track. The following section provides four key conditions that when practiced consistently build a unique culture of mutual value. Examples of organizations practicing these elements in an exceptional way are provided to support implementation in your firm. These organizations are held up not because they are perfect. Rather, they seek to be the best they can be at helping professionals learn, grow, and expand career assets. A diverse sample of firm sizes, industries, and geography were selected to illustrate that a Career Equity culture can be cultivated wherever there are thoughtful leaders who strive to make it possible. The following highlights four conditions and the companies that exemplify these best practices.

Condition 1: Link professional growth and retention to the firm's strategic plan and communicate it intentionally.

West Monroe Partners is a great example of a leadership team that is purposeful about building a culture of career significance. West Monroe Partners, or WMP, is a team of business and technical experts consulting in industries undergoing profound change. They help companies solve their most complex challenges so they can adapt, shift gears and thrive. WMP has been growing at a rapid rate. The leadership team's interest in Career Equity derived from recognition that to achieve the firm's growth plan, each firm member required a professional growth plan. This mutuality of needs is at the core of WMP's approach internally and with clients. The leadership team is keenly aware of the relationship between professional growth, retention, and business results. Helping professionals build career equity is a daily practice.

The firm has dedicated leadership resources to professional career growth and retention that are integral to the firm's strategic plan and superior to other conventional performance management systems they have used in the past. The Career Equity model provides a common language for WMP leaders and professionals to discuss shared goals and expectations. Susan Stelter, Chief Administrative Officer, articulates the firm's intention best. "We want this to be a dream job for our people, and the experience we provide will help us deliver greater value to clients."

While many Career Equity organizations utilize tools to enhance recruiting or career development, the West Monroe team has applied Career Equity tools, practices, and principles to every touch point along the career lifecycle: recruiting, onboarding, career advising, and performance management. Prior to implementing the Career Equity model, WMP leaders found it difficult to conceptualize and communicate to employees how engaging work is impactful to career satisfaction. In other words, why are challenging assignments value-added to career growth instead of something to run away from? The Career Equity model gives firm leaders a context for helping professionals diagnose the difference between a career unsatisfying experience and one that is required to hone skills and competencies in the direction of their career vision. "The firm's goal is to further embed these concepts into everything we do," said Susan. The following are just a few of the ways Career Equity has come to life at West Monroe Partners.

- Retention or average tenure of professionals has increased over 21 percent since implementation. In 2013, firm turnover, as in most professional firms, was 23 percent. Today it is 18 percent. This is a significant change for any professional services firm and has enabled WMP to develop a larger pool of potential managers and senior managers to promote when opportunities present themselves.

- More than 95 percent of partners, managers, and consultants have a written Three-Year Letter. This enables every member of the firm to clearly articulate their personal and professional goals and get support for pursuing them. This increased clarity of goals and aspirations is a key component of both increased satisfaction and retention.

- There has been a deeper involvement in the community since implementing the Career Equity model. While WMP has always been focused on helping professionals identify their passion to give back and become engaged in the community, it is now helping professionals increase their equity in Career Asset #4 – Contributing to Community and Culture. The firm has taken engagement in this area to a new level because they realize that the best professionals want to work somewhere that has a spirit and practice of giving back. Firm leaders developed the 1+1+1 initiative as part of their strategic plan. They dedicate one percent of the firm's time, one percent of the firm's talent, and one percent of the firm's financial resources annually to supporting the communities in which West Monroe practices and thrives.

Career equity is practiced as a principle not a program. Leaders helping professionals achieve sustainable growth know that results and satisfaction are not achieved by a training program

CAREER EQUITY BY THE NUMBERS

Career Equity Report Card

Subject	Baseline	1-Year Goal	3-Year Goal
% EEs (reviewed in Sept.) with Three-Year Letter	20%	93.6%	100%
% Projects with Completed Reviews	63%	77%	100%
PAM Turnover	22.2%	15.6%	< 16%
Average WMP Tenure (years) – Departures	2.1	2.8	3.5
Experienced Hire Cycle Time (days)	97	93	< 90

© West Monroe Partners (WMP)

TRAINING

258	2012 - Total trained in rollout
390	2013 - Total trained, as of Dec.
409	Total FTEs employed by WMP

CAREER ADVISOR RELATIONSHIPS

Comfort giving annual reviews

Ratings after Career Equity rollout jumped to **8.58/10**

Career advisors rated **7.44/10** prior to Career Equity rollout

RECRUITING

Over **2,000** candidates were screened using career equity-focused questions

ORIENTATION

118 New employees received orientation training with Career Equity

50 Employees that saw the career equity video in Consulting 101

EXCELLENT RELATIONSHIPS

| PRE-ROLLOUT | 75% | Reported by consultants |
| POST ROLLOUT | 91.7% | Regarding career advisors |

Source: West Monroe Partners (WMP)

or performance management initiative. The WMP purpose is guided by a desire to align a professional's aspirations to firm goals. Ultimately, this creates the virtuous cycle of more fulfilling career experiences. When WMP leaders considered implementing the Career Equity model, they hosted thoughtful conversations with the Human Resources team. They discussed how they would evaluate their effectiveness. They believed that Career Equity, like all other business strategies, needed to be measured. The dashboard on Page 137 is a result of those discussions:

Scorecard updates are communicated on a regular basis. From the beginning, WMP firm leaders understood that helping both professionals AND the firm grow meant Career Equity needed to be integrated or woven into every people-related business practice. Like other elements of organizational effectiveness, cultivating a Career Equity culture began with leadership. The WMP leaders and other successful firms achieve great people-related business results because they have a strong desire to offer professionals a unique career experience. These leaders communicate their intentions clearly, concisely, and most importantly, hold themselves accountable for making it real. For example, WMP began by educating every Career Advocate, which included managers, directors, and partners, in the Career Equity philosophy, tools, and resources. Their senior team participated in all learning sessions and crafted personal Three-Year Letters.

Every professional was invited to participate in learning workshops to equip them with tools to develop a Three-Year Letter or career vision, a Career Board of Directors, learning plans, and the confidence to share their aspirations in annual performance reviews or mentoring sessions.

How does your firm define and implement strategic goals for professional growth and development? Professionals are always testing a firm's commitment to career growth and investment. Many firm leaders say they are dedicated to professional growth, but few in practice follow through on these words with consistent action. This is especially true during uncertain economic times. The press is replete with stories of companies that abandon strategic people investments when revenue and profits shrink. While reducing time and resources in training and coaching costs seem logical, it is evidence of short-term thinking and sends a strong message about the firm's intentions that are difficult to counteract when economic times improve. Those who attract and retain talent consistently are committed to mutual career and organizational growth through all business cycles.

Another example of linking people priorities to strategic priorities comes from an organization whose success is inextricably linked to the communities they serve. When the leadership team of Northwestern Mutual in Los Angeles, Irvine, Las Vegas, and West LA, articulated a vision of winning the coveted national Northwestern Mutual Community Impact Award, it was a bold goal. Only one organization out of 75 network offices within this Fortune 100 company are recognized annually. The team was purposeful and passionate about building a culture that "gives back." Chau Le, Chief Operating Officer, believes that community engagement achieves a triple win for both professionals and the organization.

"Our firm's Mission is to inspire people to achieve their financial security dreams. When we work with Starlight Children's Foundation, and the families they serve, to combat childhood cancer, our people see how their contributions help others realize their dreams of improving children's health. In addition, each community-giving event builds a stronger sense of community and volunteerism, both internally and externally. Finally, we believe the more our people play an active role in the community, the more the community knows about the strength of Northwestern Mutual." To gain the greatest input and engagement, Chau formed a Community Service Committee. Today, the committee is made up of 16 members who represent roles across the firm including the Managing Partner, Chief Development Officer, three Managing Directors, five Financial Advisors, five Network Office staff, and two Associate Financial representatives. This diverse team spearheads community engagement opportunities and plays a key role in motivating participation across the organization. More than 115 people, or close to 40 percent of the organization, has actively fundraised, volunteered, and championed community giving. They were recognized at the Northwestern Mutual Annual Meeting for being the Top Fundraising team in the country and at the planning meeting where the aspiration was formed, Matt Plocher, Managing Partner, proudly announced that the team won the community service award they had envisioned just a few years before. The Northwestern Mutual Foundation provided a grant of $120,000 which funded the construction of a beautiful Teen Lounge at Mattel Children's Hospital UCLA, and in addition, Chau Le was recognized as a "Volunteer of the Year." To date, the team has raised $500,000 to benefit pediatric cancer.

How can your organization align the hearts and minds of your people to their desire to make a difference in the community, while advancing the firm's strategic goals? How would organizing a Community Engagement team promote better relationships internally, as well as accomplish goals externally? How can your organization align the hearts and minds of your people to their desire to make a difference in the community? Go to Plocher Group's website and check out a brief video of the team's approach and results. How intentional are your leaders about linking career growth to the firm's strategic plan? What people-related business results are you tracking and measuring? How can you follow the lead of firms like West Monroe Partners, Northwestern Mutual or ZeroDay Technology Solutions to increase the impact of your people investments?

Condition 2: Implement a systematic assessment of career satisfaction and develop action plans for improvement.

Every quarter, like clockwork, Lynn Davis, director of Human

Resources, and John Herber, managing partner of the accounting firm RubinBrown, LLP, convene their service line leaders for a review of the firm's best talent. Utilizing formal performance review data, input from Career Advocates (CA's) and mentors, firm leaders assess the career aspirations and advancement potential of their best professionals. Specific actionable observations and plans are documented, and Lynn is accountable for ensuring that strategies are fulfilled. What is the result? The firm has one of the highest retention rates for accounting professionals and a deep pipeline of future leaders. John and Lynn conduct a systematic review of talent, and consistently evaluate the mentors and advocates that surround emerging leaders. This scrutiny and review has enabled the firm to realize strategic growth goals. RubinBrown, one of the nation's leading accounting and professional consulting firms headquartered in St. Louis, Missouri, since 1952, has successfully opened offices in Kansas City, Missouri, Denver, Colorado, and most recently in Nashville, Tennessee. This type of geographic expansion is only possible when professionals have consistent and intentional conversations about how their career goals align with the firm's growth goals. RubinBrown has had a systematic commitment to career development for decades. Every member of the firm has a Career Advocate accountable for facilitating a formal career discussion twice a year and many protégés report meeting with advocates informally three to four times a year. This year, the firm is expanding and evolving the Career Advocate process into something they call Dual Career Advocates. Going forward, each individual will have two Career Advocates participate in career discussions. Managing Partner John Herber tested this process in partner career discussions and found that adding another perspective was highly productive. John learned that when two people are engaged in career discussions, accountability for goal achievement increases, professionals have an additional source of feedback and, most importantly, they feel the firm is more invested in their career aspirations. The Career Advocates also gain from this experience. They get to observe peers facilitate a discussion, offer solutions, or ask questions in a different way. In a high growth firm that is geographically dispersed, having two Career Advocates enables professionals to gain additional perspective with regard to industry and service line expertise, too. For example, a Tax manager might have an Audit and International Tax partner as Career Advocates or a technology consultant may have a Career Advocate with deep knowledge of construction and healthcare services in his/her review. RubinBrown never takes their relationships with professionals for granted. Every year a "Best Place to Work" survey is utilized to assess each professional's satisfaction with career development, firm culture, and other selected dimensions.

In addition, the firm conducts a Career Advocate satisfaction survey which enables each professional to comment on the quality and effectiveness of their Career Advocate relationships. After a series of formal Career Equity learning sessions, we conducted a survey to better understand how Career Equity concepts taught during training were coming to life in practice.

RubinBrown's results were exceptional. Ninety-seven percent of respondents reported that RubinBrown colleagues "care about me as a person," 87 percent reported having more than one mentor in the firm, and 99 percent – yes 99 percent believe the firm is highly respected in the community and is dedicated to "giving back." Does your firm have a quarterly mechanism for reviewing top talent, assigned Career Advocates or advisors that meet consistently with each firm member, and multiple mechanisms for evaluating professional career satisfaction? If not, borrow some ideas from RubinBrown's playbook and get your Career Equity culture and potential for firm growth underway.

The managing shareholder and shareholders of law firm Capes, Sokol, Goodman, & Sarachan, P.C., take building a Career Equity culture seriously. In addition to linking professional growth and retention to their strategic objectives, they do a great job of systematically surveying professionals to identify how the firm is doing at delivering career value for continuous improvement. Like several Career Equity advocate firms, CSGS adapted the Career Equity survey in Chapter 1 to include questions most relevant to their goals.

On Page 146 and 147 is a sample of CSGS semi-annual Career Equity survey. This can create a higher degree of ownership and accountability for firm leaders when making decisions about areas of improvement. The CSGS shareholders have been systematically using the same survey for several years and now have a great baseline to evaluate organizational strengths and opportunities for improvement.

After collecting responses through an anonymous electronic survey, the results are reviewed in detail by the managing partner and shareholders. The managing partner hosts a career development forum to share results with all associates and paralegals to identify priorities for action. What process does your organization use to systematically measure professional career satisfaction? What happens to feedback gathered? How do you know if you are making progress?

Condition 3: Ensure every professional has a Trusted Career Advisor or mechanism for feedback.

No Career Equity element is more essential to creating an effective culture for professionals than the presence of caring and challenging mentors or what I call "Trusted Career Advisors." Research on professional growth, development, retention, and advancement never fails to spotlight the importance of these career confidants. As mentioned earlier, left to their own devices most professionals seek out guidance from friends and peers. While emotional support from peers is comforting, career coaching from peers lacks several important components. First, peers, especially early in their career, lack sufficient experience or perspective to provide a long-term solution. In other words, they do not have the benefit of repetitive practice or consistent implementation.

Second, peer relationships are often focused more on support than on challenge. To advance a significant goal in any area, but especially in one's career, means doing things that are uncom-

Capes, Sokol, Goodman, & Sarachan
Career Equity Firm Survey

1. Which of the following best describes your position at the Firm:

2. Please indicate your current satisfaction with the following elements of Engaging and Challenging Work at CSGS:

A. The role I play in client cases gives me an opportunity to learn and grow.

B. I have a high degree of diversity in my work experiences, cases, and projects.

C. I have a high degree of autonomy and flexibility in accomplishing my work.

D. I receive timely and relevant feedback regarding my performance.

3. Please indicate the extent to which the following dimensions of Meaningful Relationships are available to you at CSGS:

A. The practice group(s) I work with promote(s) collaborative decision-making.

B. Other shareholders appreciate and recognize my contributions.

C. The practice chair, in the area I work most often, sets clear expectations and goals.

D. Other shareholders indicate an interest in my career goals and aspiration.

E. I am intentional about developing meaningful relationships at the firm.

**Capes, Sokol, Goodman, & Sarachan
Career Equity Firm Survey, continued**

4. Please indicate the extent to which the following dimensions of Professional Learning and Growth are available to you at CSGS:

A. I have adequate technology and tools to accomplish my work.

B. My firm invests in my professional growth.

C. I am encouraged to participate in professional organizations (e.g., Bar Association, etc.).

D. The firm has an effective process for identifying and developing future leaders.

E. I am encouraged to invest time and "give back" to community and non-profit organizations.

F. The firm's size and growth provide ample opportunities for professional growth.

5. Please indicate the extent to which you agree with the following elements of building a strong and unique CSGS culture:

A. The firm's mission and values are discussed frequently.

B. The firm has a positive reputation in the community.

C. Retention of the best talent is a firm priority.

D. Recruiting the best talent is a firm priority.

E. Firm investments in marketing and public relations are advancing the CSGS brand.

6. What is the ONE thing (there may be many strengths) CSGS is best at?

7. What is the ONE thing you think demands attention and action?

fortable. Trusted advisors, with experience and authority, can help push professionals out of their comfort zone to realize the next level of growth. Finally, and most importantly, peers lack the authority to influence needed change. For example, if an employee is dissatisfied with the repetitive nature of their assignments, peers do not have the organizational authority to change those assignments. A manager or mentor does. Based on my research, without purposeful and planned support from caring leaders, your best professionals run the risk of getting bad career advice 60 percent of the time.

Design Group is a premier engineering and technology solutions provider, serving the world's leading consumer products, life sciences, and industrial manufacturing clients. The firm operates as an independent and autonomous division of Barry-Wehmiller companies, a $2 billion technology and manufacturing company which is comprised of more than 60 acquired companies and over 8,000 team members around the world. But Barry-Wehmiller is more than just a successful capital equipment and engineering solutions firm. The company takes pride in its Truly Human Leadership™ culture, and a leadership philosophy built upon the principles of People, Purpose, and Performance. By providing meaningful work in an environment of care and compassion, Barry-Wehmiller seeks to build a better world through sending its team members home feeling fulfilled and appreciated. Design Group has grown substantially since its formation 30 years ago. Today the firm provides professional services through over 1000 engineering and technical specialists in more than 30 offices across the United States. Managing Partner, Joe Wilhelm and his leadership team, adopted the Career Equity model in 2007 as a platform to enhance professional development, career growth, and retention. Joe and his team believe that having strong internal career advisors is essential to the firm and its professional growth. Joe attributes Career Equity, a vibrant people-centric culture, and strong operating disciplines as the core elements which led the firm to achieve 15 percent compounded annual growth rate (CAGR) over a span of 10 years. The 35 Design Group Partners are committed and intentional about replicating and sustaining Career Equity fundamentals across all of the firm's offices. I checked in with Joe to discuss how the Career Equity principles are working today. "Career Equity continues to be a foundational element of our Career Development Discussion (CDD) process ... and every new Design Group professional is schooled in this concept as part of their onboarding process. We have an extensive internal website dedicated to this process for our professionals, including courses, webinars, and personal instruction." Below is an excerpt from the Design Group Career Equity homepage.

Career Equity is a concept designed to help our professionals grow in their careers. Career Equity is defined as "the professional's stake, or equity, which is being built as their career develops." The

Career Development Discussion (CDD) focuses on linking your daily activities, your investment of time and effort, and the firm's investment in you to the development of your personal career equity. We believe that as you increase your career equity, you will be able to increase the value of your contributions to the firm, and help build your stake in the future!

There are five main attributes that indicate how engaged a professional is in "actively developing" his or her own personal career equity: 1) Is the professional engaged in meaningful and challenging work? 2) Is the professional developing meaningful relationships internally and externally? 3) Is the professional learning and growing with each assignment? 4) Is the professional involved from a community or culture standpoint? 5) Is the professional recognized and rewarded fairly based on their contributions?

One of the main focuses of the Career Development Discussion is to highlight how engaged professionals are in the development of their career equity. Through the CDD, professionals rate their own level of engagement; they are not rated by a manager. Professionals have the opportunity to assess their current position with their manager and explore their potential for additional growth opportunities. Through improved career planning facilitated by the CDD, the firm and the professional work together to advance career equity in harmony with advancing the goals of the firm."

The Career Equity and CDD process works extraordinarily well for new employees, especially those early in their professional careers. Caleb Lambert is a perfect example of Career

Equity in action at the Design Group. Caleb started with the firm as a co-op student from Missouri University of Science and Technology in mechanical engineering. One of the reasons Caleb accepted a full-time offer with the Design Group in 2012 was their commitment to the mutual career growth of professionals. In his short tenure, Caleb has received multiple forms of recognition. Last year, he received the firm's PRIDE Award given to professionals who have made meaningful contributions toward client development through their direct or indirect actions, and prior to that he received the Design Group's High Five Award for professionals that go above and beyond their normal daily duties to achieve client success. Caleb clearly understands how to help

Note to self: strong career development cultures attract and retain the best interns and talent.

clients succeed, but like most Career Equity builders, what is striking about Caleb is his passion for mentoring and developing others.

Caleb's advice to other professionals is this: "Take responsibility for your career growth and come prepared to mentoring meetings. When I am well prepared for a mentoring meeting I feel good about clearly communicating my intentions. It also enables me to examine how what I want aligns with the goals of the firm." The reciprocal component of Career Equity, or the fit between his needs and the needs of the firm, is a tangible asset for Caleb. He is also mindful that reciprocity is required in effective mentoring relationships. This is a good reminder as you evaluate your firm's mentoring program or consider implementing one. As Caleb shares, "The best mentors need to take initiative for periodic contact beyond formal career discussions with their professionals."

"From my experience what really drives results is a mentor who offers continual contact. At times, even mentors who are strongly committed to the career growth of others can get bogged down with other job requirements. Having continual contact, outside of Career Equity discussions, helps mentors keep professionals focused on the goals that matter most and leave professionals feeling that someone really cares about their development." The result of this proactive thinking and effort is this: Caleb earned a promotion this year and will be moving toward the role of facilitating Career Development Discussions for others. How does your firm empower professionals to build their career and initiate discussions with managers or mentors about growth and satisfaction? What could you learn from a conversation with your best people?

Another example of an organization that ensures its members have a Trusted Career Advisor or mechanism for feedback is Saint Louis University's John Cook School of Business. The John Cook School of Business has a long-standing history of creating successful business leaders. It is the oldest business school west of the Mississippi River and offers highly ranked business programs. It is in the Top 10 for Entrepreneurship and International Business Programs and in the Top 100 of all MBA programs in the world. One component of the School's success is purposeful career advising services. The Director of Career Resources Center at the Business School, Barb Gradala, is very intentional about offering students tools and resources that are relevant, can be consistently utilized to advance their career goals, and optimize post-graduate career opportunities. Barb was intrigued by the Career Equity model and, more specifically, the Career Board of Directors concept as a solution to help students think more strategically about their relationships, see networking as a purposeful activity, and develop a new platform to explore their career aspirations.

Since 2009, I have been working with Barb to offer MBA students a Career Board of Directors workshop. The results are inspiring, For example, one student who was recruited by a corporate investment bank in Switzerland, recognized that the Career Board of Directors concept could help her build stronger relationships during her on-boarding process and in the high potential program.

Another student, Daryl, shared that the Career Board gives him more confidence in decision-making and evaluating potential positions. "My Board helps me catch things and think about perspectives that I don't." Daryl sees the importance of having diverse individuals representing different segments, industries, and experience levels available to him as career advisors. Finally, another student named Alexy realized that the Career Board enabled him to develop a long-term vision for networking. Networking was not about meeting someone one time at an event, but a way to engage with other business leaders and professionals for longer term mutual growth. These are just a few of the testimonials Barb has heard from students who participate in the workshop. Barb and Saint Louis University's School of Business are very intentional about equipping students with practical tools that lead to greater personal responsibility and results in their careers. How could your organization leverage the Career Board of Directors concept to promote diverse viewpoints and foster better communication between trusted career advisors and employees?

As mentioned earlier, Northwestern Mutual Financial Network is the only company to lead its industry as one of America's Most Admired Companies® for nearly 30 consecutive years. The organization's business model is totally dependent on recruiting and retaining the best talent in the financial-security industry. Therefore, firm leaders are purposeful about the support and challenge each financial representative receives to fulfill his or her career aspirations. The Plocher Group is the #1 Northwestern Mutual agency in the United States. They deploy multiple mentoring strategies to foster professional growth and retention (e.g., mentors, monthly client builder meetings, regular coaching from managing directors, etc.). One of the best examples of a systematic mentoring process is their Quarterly Board of Review. Managing Partner, Matt Plocher, ensures that each financial representative has the opportunity for a review by a Board that comprises the managing director, mentor(s), and the firm's development director. This group meets four times a year to review the professional's progress toward his or her business and career aspirations for the current fiscal year as well as his or her long-term vision. Each professional is required to present a report of his or her plan, goals, and results. Feedback from the Board is documented and forms the basis for monthly coaching and development. This highly customized and consistent forum for feedback is a unique and valued strategy for adding Career Equity to each professional's career portfolio.

Condition 4: Instill a habit of relentless follow-up and follow-through on career aspirations.

Benjamin Franklin is known for saying "well done is better than well said." In cultivating an organizational culture, this could not be more true and relevant. Research by Jim Collins, internationally known author of *Good to Great,* reveals the best organizations achieve great results because their leaders execute strategy consistently. Leaders who desire short-term success can put this book down. You will not achieve the multiple benefits a Career Equity culture delivers. Only those who have the capacity to delay gratification and the confidence to persist in the face of doubt truly succeed.

What mechanism does your organization use to help your best professionals follow-up on their aspirations? Many organizations implement processes which invite professionals to set lofty goals, but few cultivate a discipline of relentlessly reviewing these results. As mentioned in Chapter 7, research by Dr. Gail Matthews, a professor in Dominican's Department of Psychology in the School of Arts, Humanities and Social Sciences, found that more than 70 percent of people who reported weekly goal updates achieved higher levels compared to those who did not review goals consistently. Without organizational systems and processes to support goal review, predictable career development and advancement is unlikely. The Keeley Companies, a dynamic, creative, and nationwide provider of construction, infrastructure and technology solutions, offered through three distinct business units, are relentless about the pursuit of mutual growth for their businesses and leaders. Each organization has held two strategic planning forums (STP meetings) annually for the past 10 years; one at the beginning of the business cycle and one at mid-year. The purpose of these forums is to review each leader's individual progress toward a three to five year vision and current year's goals.

Goals must include a written commitment by each leader to complete at least 40 hours of personal/professional learning and growth. Each leader presents his/her plan and receives personalized feedback about what is going well and areas for improvement. In addition to these bi-annual forums, the President of each operating company has a monthly "Review of Results" with each company leader to ensure goals and action plans remain on track and in alignment throughout the year. Finally, the company provides an external coach or advisor to meet with leaders individually to discuss career development and ensure each is staying focused on longer-term career aspirations. Just ask Rusty Keeley, Chief Executive Officer of the Keeley Companies, about the results of relentlessly reviewing goals. In 2004, the combined Keeley Companies revenue was $42 million. In 2015 after multiple years of implementing this intentional goal review, along with a lot of hard work, the combined revenue was $225 million; an increase of $183 million or 432.66 percent growth. As a result, the company has been recognized as one of the fastest growing companies by the St. Louis Business Journal, and Rusty recently received the prestigious Entrepreneur of the Year Award from Ernst & Young.

"A goal is a dream with action plans and a deadline," Rusty says. "Our strategic planning process is scalable and has accountability at its core. It is non-negotiable for our leadership team because I believe a team that develops clear goals together, buys in together, and reviews goals together achieves more success. Our success rises and falls on our ability to hire, develop and retain top talent. Our Strategic Planning (STP) process provides each leader with the feedback and support needed to achieve individual goals and, therefore, we achieve ours. Our culture of #keeleycares centers on this philosophy and practice."

Finally, the Fellows Program of the St. Louis Business Diversity Initiative (SLBDI) is an incredible career development and advancement organization for high-performing leaders of color. Now moving into its 10th year, as the flagship program of the SLBDI, the Fellows program offers more than 66 Fellows from more than 40 of St. Louis's top companies and organizations (e.g., Emerson, MasterCard, Ameren, Boeing, etc.) a unique leadership and learning experience.

To date, more than 500 diverse leaders have completed the program. This yearlong experience focuses on professional/ leadership development, civic engagement, and relationship building. While a Building Career Equity workshop is part of the Fellows curriculum, it is the multiple touch points in its design and the impressive results that make the program note-worthy. The Fellows Program includes managers and sponsors with opportunities to play an active role in the development of the Fellows they sponsor. For example, two open sessions on Leading with Inclusion and Creating Partnerships across Boundaries invite participants and their managers to learn together. The Initiative measures the outcomes of each Fellow's cohort and the results are impressive. More than 63.9 percent of Fellows are promoted and/or their responsibilities increased after completing the program (Source: Annual Fellows Alumni survey).

Zundra Bryant, Business Leader, MasterCard Global Shared Services Center, Fellow of the class of 2009, and a member of the Fellow's advisory board, shared how the Fellow's experience shaped her career growth and development. Zundra's guidance to future candidates and leaders is this: "You are worth the investment. Participating in the Fellows program was a life-changing experience that magnified the trajectory of my personal and professional aspirations. I gained exposure to incredible instructors who imparted knowledge to guide me through deep introspection and reflection that has helped me make meaningful life decisions and has had a significant impact on my family, friends, colleagues and many others. Most importantly my definition of success is no longer shaped by outward pressures, but from my own determination of my unique value and purpose."

How does your organization develop future leaders of color? How are their managers and leaders encouraged to be participants in the process? What are the outcomes you are achieving?

The purpose of this chapter is to equip firm leaders with the knowledge, tools and examples to begin cultivating a Career Equity culture. While the elements of Career Equity are consistent, the way each organization embraces and implements these practices vary widely. Creating a Career Equity culture is not a cookie-cutter effort. When implemented thoughtfully it will enhance the uniqueness of a culture and differentiate your firm in an increasingly competitive marketplace for talent. One of the best ways to get culture building underway is to ask firm leaders and professionals to complete the Career Equity Culture Assessment. Host a series of discussions about where your firm is today and which elements would make a significant difference to the career growth and satisfaction of professionals. Full culture change can take between three and five years. Set realistic expectations, organize a plan, and begin.

Extra Credit for Firm Leaders:

1) Read *Aligning the Stars,* Jay W. Lorsh and Thomas J. Tierney, (Boston: Harvard Business School Publishing, 2002).

2) Consult *Managing the Professional Services Firm,* David Maister's, (New York: Free Press Paperbacks: A Division of Simon and Schuster Inc., 1993).

3) Read *Good to Great,* Jim Collins, (New York: HarperCollins Publishers Inc., 2001).

Conclusions

"Success is a journey, not a destination. The doing is often more important than the outcome."

—*Arthur Ashe*

uilding Career Equity, like life, is not a linear journey. Whether you are exploring these practices for yourself, your protégé(s), or have aspirations of building a Career Equity culture for your firm, the process begins with self-awareness and demands collaboration. Greater awareness lies in taking the time to answer fundamental questions about your career. For example, where have you accumulated the most career assets? What is energizing or easy for you? What needs a higher level of intention? How can you more fully realize your potential and make a difference in the lives of others? If you take nothing else away from this book, I hope you see career growth and satisfaction as an interdependent process. No one achieves success in isolation. Career Equity master builders have a clear vision of where they want to go and work purposefully with clients, colleagues, leaders, and community organizations to make their vision a reality. Their stories, in retrospect, may sound logical and straightforward. If you do A, then B will follow. In truth, everyone mentioned in this book, individually or organizationally, achieved success because they persisted in the face of delay, disappointment, and often rejection. At the same time, they sought feedback from people who cared about their growth and challenged them to do things that were neither comfortable nor familiar. They are building rich and rewarding careers because they never gave up. They also sought help in the pursuit of their aspirations.

Career Equity builders are experts at making and keeping commitments. They know that career significance is achieved over the long-term. They defy the current culture of instant gratification.

They have their eye on a horizon of three to five years, not three to five months. Time and time again, the most effective people I know say that their most valuable career experiences are the most difficult ones. When confronted with a difficult situation, manager, or peer, they often thought of leaving or quitting. The difference is that they did not.

Thus, one piece of evidence we see in the histories of Career Equity builders is tenure. What does your résumé communicate about your career? Does it reveal serial changes? At the turn of the 21st Century, frequent job changes were perceived to be a badge of honor. But like the dot.com bubble, that career strategy burst.

When you look at those who build significant careers, businesses, and lives, you will see a pattern of what one highly successful managing partner calls "long obedience in the same direction." Of course there are exceptions to every rule and factors beyond our control, but in the end, those who realize great satisfaction and impact stay for the time required to make a difference. Tenure is not a reflection of complacency or fear about leaving. Instead, it is a thoughtful decision aligned to long-term aspirations. As career opportunities arise, Career Equity builders consider how it will fit into their overall portfolio of experiences, relationships, and rewards. Like the "buy and hold" philosophy of financial investing, building Career Equity demands a plan and commitment to stay the course in turbulent times.

The five factors of Building Career Equity provide the road map for achieving a long-term return on your investment of time, talent, and energy. In summary, Doing Engaging Work provides the framework for defining our aspirations and vision. The tools and practices in Chapter 2 help identify the skills and experiences that motivate us and provide a filter for evaluating potential career opportunities.

In Chapter 3, we discover how and why meaningful relationships influence our success and the strategies necessary to cultivate more of the interactions we want. Few professionals stay committed to their career or organization without planned and purposeful learning. Therefore, Chapter 4 outlines five strategies for actively managing a learning and development plan that keeps curiosity high and career assets current. Is giving back to the broader context of human affairs or community vital to you? Chapter 5 offers tools, examples, and inspiration for how to get involved while building career capacity. A purposeful career strategy, relationships, learning, and giving have their rewards. Chapter 6 provides specific recommendations on how to increase the return on career investments by knowing the facts about salary, benefits, and opportunities for recognition.

While the five assets of Building Career Equity provide a powerful mental model and practical tools, it is the intentional implementation or "doing" as Arthur Ashe notes that makes the difference. If you struggle with following through on your career ambitions, re-read Chapter 7, Putting Action and Accountability Behind Aspirations. Does one habit speak to you? Commit to utilize it for the next 30 days. Chapter 8 was written specifically to and for firm leaders. It offers a toolkit for collaborating with professionals the organization most wants to attract and retain. Companies recognized as "best places to work" generously share how they implement the Building Career Equity formula. They have evidence of positive business results when they focus on helping professionals realize their career aspirations.

"Boldness has genius, power, and magic in it. Only engage, and then the mind grows heated. Begin it, and the work will be completed."

—*Johann Wolfgang von Goethe*

What is the first step you can take to act on this knowledge and learning? Who can help you convert dreams into tangible career experiences? What would it be like if everyone in your organization had a shared way of defining, discussing, and advancing their career goals?

I would value hearing from you about how Building Career Equity has formed your career goals, aspirations, and, most importantly, action. Visit BuildingCareerEquity.com to share your success stories.

Bibliography

Allen, David. *Getting Things Done.* New York: Penguin Group, 2001.

Babcock, Linda, and Sarah Laschever. *Women Don't Ask: Negotiation and the Gender Divide.* Princeton University Press, 2003.

Baker, Wayne E. *Achieving Success through Social Capital.* Jossey-Bass: August 2000.

Birlingham, Bo. "The Believer." New York: *Inc.* magazine, August 2008.

Boldt, Lawrence G. *How to Find the Work You Love.* New York: Penguin Group, 1996.

Buckingham, Marcus and Donald O. Clifton. *Now Discover Your Strengths.* New York: The Free Press, 2001.

Butler, Timothy and James Waldroop. *Discovering Your Career in Business.* New York: Perseus Books, 1996.

Chapman, Bob and Sisodia, Raj. *Everybody Matters: The Extraordinary Power of Caring For Your People Like Family.* Penguin Random House, 2015.

Covert, Jack and Todd Satterson. *The 100 Best Business Books of All Time: What They Say, Why They Matter, And How They Can Help You.* New York: Penguin Group, 2009.

Covey, Stephen R. *The Seven Habits of Highly Effective People.* New York: Free Press of Simon & Shuster, 2004.

Covey, Stephen R. and Bob Whitman, Breck England. *Predictable Results in Unpredictable Times.* Salt Lake City, Utah: Franklin Covey, September 2009.

Csíkszentmihályi, Mihály. Flow: *The Psychology of Optimal Experience.* Harper Perennial Modern Classics: July 2008.

Drucker, Peter. *The Practice of Management.* New York: Harper Collins Publishers, Inc. October 1954.

Fischer, Donna. *People Power: 12 Power Principles to Enrich your Business, Career, & Personal Networks.* Marietta, Georgia: Bard Press, 1995.

Forni, P.M. *Choosing Civility: The Twenty-five Rules of Considerate Conduct.* New York: St. Martin's Press, February 2002.

Gladwell, Malcolm. *The Tipping Point: How Little Things Can Make A Big Difference.* Little, Brown and Company, March 2000.

Granovetter, Mark. *Getting a Job: A Study of Contacts and Careers.* University Of Chicago Press: March 1995.

Gray, Albert E. N. *The New Common Denominator of Success.* Books2Wealth Edition, Albany, OR: Albany Publishing Company, 2010.

Gualdoini, Claire. *The Greater Good: How Philanthropy Drives the American Economy and Can Save Capitalism.* New York: Times Books, 2003.

BIBLIOGRAPHY

Hill, Napolean. *Think and Grow Rich*. The Random House Publishing Group: 1937.

Kristie, James. "Boards at Their Best." *Board Room Briefing*, Winter, 2006.

Maister, David H. and Charles H. Green, and Robert M. Galford. *The Trusted Advisor*. New York: Touchstone, 2001.

Maxwell, John C. *Leadership Promises for Every Day*. Nashville, TN: Thomas J. Nelson Inc., 2003.

Rosenberg, Arthur D. *101 Ways to Stand Out at Work: How to Get the Recognition and Rewards You Deserve*. Adams Media and F+W Media Company, 2009.

Acknowledgements

The first edition of Career Equity was published in 2011. Five years later, it is energizing and affirming to see how hundreds of firms and individuals have benefitted from reading, implementing and teaching the concepts to others. Without their work the second edition is not possible.

I remain thankful to the partners and professionals of Arthur Andersen without whom this concept would not have been realized or developed. More than 14 years after the firm's exodus, due to the Enron controversy, Career Equity lives on. The end of Andersen provided an unintended context for testing how career-minded professionals adapt and adjust. The vast majority of Andersen partners and employees found engaging work, meaningful relationships, and realized career goals in new places that in 2002 were not anticipated. They are a continuing inspiration and example of how building career equity comes to life.

I want to express my gratitude to progressive and forward thinking firms like West Monroe Partners, Rubin Brown, Barry-Wehmiller's Design Group, Northwestern Mutual, ZeroDay Technology Solutions and leaders like Bob Chapman, Gary Beu, John Herber, Lynn Davis, Michael Lewis, Rusty Keeley, Paul Montello and Matt Plocher. Like most organizational development efforts without strong leadership effective implementation and meaningful results are not possible. They are my heroes. To professionals like Tasha, Jon, Corey, Susan, Caleb and Zundra who were willing to share their stories so that others might learn and grow. I salute your commitment to the career equity principles. You represent the essence of "meaningful relationships." No book can be realized without the help and support of capable editors and publishing professionals.

Wendy Werner and Patience Schock provided invaluable editorial expertise. Additionally, Wendy's vigilant research of the facts ensured support of key theories. To Peggy Nehmen, who has been a guiding force on creative design and book promotion and publishing since the beginning. As I learned from Dr. Ana Fels, no significant goal is achieved without an appreciative audience. I am thankful to my husband Joe for his ongoing support and encouragement of my professional goals.

Here's to all that seek to learn and embrace Career Equity stories, practices, and tool for the purpose of achieving mutual growth.